D1195399

SELECTED ESSAYS AND CRITICAL
WRITINGS OF A. R. ORAGE

A. R. Orage

SELECTED ESSAYS

AND

CRITICAL WRITINGS

EDITED BY

HERBERT READ AND

DENIS SAURAT

Essay Index Reprint Series

BOOKS FOR LIBRARIES PRESS, INC.
FREEPORT, NEW YORK

First Published 1935
Reprinted 1967

LIBRARY OF CONGRESS CATALOG NUMBER:
67-30225

PRINTED IN THE UNITED STATES OF AMERICA

CONTENTS

I

THE ART OF READING

I

THE ART OF READING

ON STYLE

A good many of the obscurities of literary criticism or the judgement of writing would be removed if only it were remembered that literature is a substitute for speech. Ages before the invention of script, men communicated with each other in the medium of words, and not on everyday occasions and everyday subjects only, but on special occasions and upon subjects of the whole range of human interest. For these special occasions, moreover, the form of the spoken communication was adapted both in respect of subject and style. Occasions of entertainment necessitated light and easy narrative forms, varying in length from the *conte* to the *histoire*. Historic occasions called for recollections in the form of biography, episode and epic. Solemn occasions or occasions of crisis demanded the religious narrative, intercession or ceremony, or appeals of the nature of oratory. There is scarcely a literary form now existing that was not cultivated and brought to a high degree of perfection ages before the invention of letters and the printing press.

However much else has been changed by the invention of a script for speech, it is obvious that the natural, original and fundamental relationship of ancient illiterate times differs in no important respect from the writer-reader relationship of literate ages. Now, as then, on the one side is a man employing words for the purpose of communicating his thoughts and feelings to others; and now, as then, on the other side are men predisposed by the fact of their presence and attention to receive and to be affected by the thoughts and feelings thus communicated to them. That this ancient relationship stands, indeed, fundamentally unchanged by all the changes due to printing is proved by this alone: that writing is everywhere acknowledged to be at its highest and best when it most closely reproduces the living presence of its author—in short, when it speaks.

The judgement applied by hearers to speakers in the ages before printing was, however, an act rather than an art. No art-criticism, in fact, was needed in presence of the speaker himself. His hearers judged him exactly as they were in the instinctive habit of judging everybody else. He was forcible, he was grand, he was impressive, he was entertaining, in precisely the same way in which their own familiars were. Furthermore, they had not to search the archives of his life for light upon his meaning. He was there before them in the flesh and everything he had to say was insensibly received by them in the light of his visible presence and personality. It was impossible to persuade them that they ought to give him their attention because of his reputation or the originality of his style, or for any of the hundred and one reasons that an audience of hearers to-day is besought to read what is intrinsically distasteful. The ancients were all in this respect from Missouri; and the sight and sound of the speaker's living presence was the first and last criterion they employed for their judgement of the value of his communication. The man was the style.

Though, as I have said, the fundamental relationship remained unchanged with the introduction of printing, nevertheless the technique of the relationship has been greatly transformed. At opposite ends of the situation stand to-day the same two original figures, a speaker and a hearer;

but, in place of the former direct and sensible communication between man and man, there is to-day the whole contrivance of printing; type has been substituted for voice.

At first glance it might appear that the difference thus introduced was merely mechanical, and that all that was needed was to record in script the words as uttered by the speaker. Naïve writers are still under the impression that a transcript of life is obtained by transcribing utterances textually. But this overlooks the fact that of the total presence of the speaker in person, his actual words are only a partial representation; and a thousand subtleties indiscoverable in the verbatim report of his speech were clearly perceived by his hearers in the light of his presence. Recall Æschines reading in exile the oration of Demosthenes that condemned him, and deploring that it gave only a faint impression of its effect when Demosthenes delivered it. And Æschines was no mean orator himself. The transition from speaking to writing, from hearing to reading, demanded more, in short, than simply a script for the words; it demanded the addition to the verbal text of substitutes for all the rest of the living speaker's obvious properties, his gestures, his eyes, his movements, his whole personality. The conveyance, within the verbal framework of literature, of the man himself, apart from and over and above his mere words, is what is truly defined as style. In literature, the style is the man.

Unfortunately, with all our reading, the majority of readers are still naïve in their judgements of the man as revealed in his work. Though in truth there is always a man behind the work—be the work of any literary form—but in addition to being behind the work, he is also, by the agency of style, within the work as well, yet, thanks to the fact that our judgement of a man as writer is not instinctive like our judgements of men as men, but requires to be cultivated precisely because the style in question is necessarily cultivated, readers who would not be deceived as hearers for a single moment go hopelessly wrong in their judgement of speakers when disguised as writers. Not only are they carried away in the effects of the text upon themselves, but their true judgement of the value and significance of the writer as man is lost—sometimes never to be found—in their inability to look for the man in his work.

THE TRUE REALISM

True realism, or creation in the spirit of Nature, is two-formed. One kind divines the potential reality, and the other divines the intention. Prolific and multifarious as Nature is, her course is still only one among a thousand possible. Of all the routes by which man has been reached, was the actual route taken the only conceivable? There may have been—and possibly there were—many other routes begun and abandoned before the route actual was finally determined. The first form of imaginative realism has its sphere here: it divines what Nature could an she would: what, in fact, might have been or still may be (for life is not over yet). And the second form has its sphere in the world of the actual becoming. What Nature not only *can*, but has a mind to—this is the material of the realism of the second order.

The pitch is high, but by no means too high for the dignity of literature. Nothing is more depressing to a critic than to witness the ease with which writers of no creative ability whatever reach by acclamation a 'front rank'. They have only to copy Nature slavishly to be greeted as creative artists. But to copy Nature is one of the easiest things in the world. At least ten thousand reporters do it daily. From every war-front 'realist' descriptions of battle arrive by mail that no professional 'realist' writer could equal. Tolstoy,

Zola, Stephen Crane, were absolutely beaten at their own game by many a casual soldier writing home to a sympathetic friend. If a description of what is, of so-called actuality, be the final aim of literature, we ought to flatter ourselves that pretty well anybody can reach it. There is nothing in the literary profession to brag about or to call for special respect. Our novelists only differ from our rank and file by reason of their greater leisure and lesser experiences. Literature is reduced to nothing of importance.

The true realism, on the other hand, raises literature to a great art again. No mere record of experience, however novel, here obtains an entrance. Admission is by divination, not by description. Compare, for instance, the descriptions of battles in Homer and in the *Mahabharata* with the descriptions of actuality. The latter are accurate, but the former are true. There never was such a battle as Vyasa described in the *Mahabharata*. Let us hope there never will be. But, as we read it, we feel that Nature has dreamed it, and only *not* actualized it because she had other plans. By this means, actuality itself becomes transfigured; experience is given a solace; and no mere reporting can accomplish that. What is the satisfaction in knowing that such and such a thing occurred? But there is a satisfaction in knowing that it occurred as a consequence of a choice among many alternatives! Freedom is given back to us. At each moment we stand at a new crossroads. The road Nature takes will be, in course of time, the actual; the roads she passes will remain the potential. The more of all of them there are, the richer life has become for us.

'When I read the Song of Deborah,' Coleridge said, 'I never think that she is a poet, although I think the song itself a sublime poem.' Why is this remark just? The answer is to be found in the remark of Aristotle that 'of all works of art, those are the most excellent wherein chance has the least to do'. But for the chance of her exploit, Deborah would have remained dumb. But for the chance of their experiences most travellers would never have written a line of literature. But for the chance of this or that, the material of our novelists would never have fallen their way. They are as dependent upon chance as any reporter sent out of a morning to pick up a 'story'. There is no art in it, no creation: it is simply luck.

That, in spite of the multitude of creative artists among us, there is no creation is evident from this fact; that, outside of a few figures (Sherlock Holmes is the most notable) not a character in modern fiction has leapt out of its book into life. Dickens, by contrast, seems to have been a veritable master in Nature's workshop. He seems to have watched Nature at work, to have acquired her trick, and to have bettered her instruction. The London of his day certainly afforded Nature an opportunity for ingenious creation; but even Life was not more inventive than Dickens. At the same time he is vastly inferior to Shakespeare and the major artists. It is true he worked in the spirit of Nature, but as her assistant, not as her prophet and seer. What Nature could do and was already doing, Dickens could do as well as she. But what Nature was still striving to do, and as yet could not actualize, Shakespeare did in imagination in advance of her. Shakespeare created more easily than Nature, while Dickens created only as easily as Nature. Look at Falstaff. What approximations to him Nature has made and, let us hope, is still making! There was no holding up the mirror to Nature when Shakespeare created Falstaff. Rather it was the holding up of a telescope to Nature! Dickens never held up a mirror (as our 'realists' do); nor did he hold up a telescope; but his mind was a kaleidoscope.

THE NOBLEST USE OF WRITING

Isocrates, Milton's 'old man eloquent', composed speeches he never delivered himself, but which when delivered by others produced the very effects he had intended. What a marvellous 'sense' of the public mind of Athens he must have had! Similarly, every 'popular' writer of to-day has a 'sense' of his readers' minds, which betokens a high degree of intuition. So much we must allow. But then, it is much easier to write acceptably what is pleasing to your readers than what is unpleasing. We are not critical of the form in which flattery is expressed. All the more skill, therefore, is necessary to convey, and not merely to express, ideas that are likely for any reason to be resisted by our readers. The more honour when we have succeeded. Little need be thought of a writer who succeeds in conveying popular ideas to his readers: and only a little more of the writer who simply expresses unpopular ideas and cares no further whether his readers take them or leave them. Our highest admiration is reserved for the writer who both expresses and conveys salutary truths which were at the outset unpopular. To accomplish this is the noblest use of the art of writing. Every other use of the art is utilitarian or dilettante.

Two qualities, again, are necessary to this: a love amounting to a passion for conveying the ideas—and this implies a love of the minds to which they are to be conveyed; and a discrimination of words and phrases which resembles, though it much surpasses, the discrimination the musician must exercise on sounds. Words and phrases are more than notes of music: they must express ideas as well as create the atmosphere in which the ideas can be conveyed. And the smallest error is sufficient to destroy the intended effect.

We may well tremble with humility as we write; for is it not clear that we shall never arrive at the goal thus set? It is more than a life's work.

THE UTILITY OF LITERATURE

Why are we readers and writers? Assuming as an axiom the definition of man (there are few men yet) as the truth-seeking creature, the further assumption must be made that since literature everywhere and always, by the acknow-ledged best minds of the race, is reckoned as honourable, literature in some way or other is a valuable instrument of truth. But in what way precisely? I have the disadvantage of being uncertain as to the facts of the following illustration, but it may nevertheless serve. They tell me that for the ex-traction of gold from quartz a new method, called the cyanide process, has been invented, by means of which the labour of the former method of crushing and washing has been considerably reduced. Be that as it may, in theory at any rate, literature is a cyanide process applied to experience for the extraction therefrom of truth. Not all experience is of value to man as the truth-seeking creature; but only such experience as contains truth. And of this, again, on the one hand, there is so little, and, on the other hand, the means of extracting truth from it are so difficult, that, without special good fortune or specially effective methods of extraction, a man may well live a dozen lives and yet learn little to his immortal advantage. It is the function of litera-ture to communalize the particularly auriferous experiences of the fortunate (no man deserves to be called a literary man who is not, by nature, superlatively experiencing); and, at the same time, to demonstrate by example the most effective means of extracting truth from experience. Take any great book you please. Its two characteristics are, first, that it contains the record of the experiences of a rare and powerful mind; and, second, that it indicates in its method the means by which the writer turned his experiences to the account of truth. And we, the readers, by sympathetic following of him, are thus doubly instructed: in the first instance, by sharing in his experiences; and, in the second, by learning a means of turning our own to account. But is this not enough to establish the utility—yes, the utility—of literature—utility being here defined as something that is useful to man as the truth-seeker?

WHAT WORDS DO

The dismissal of honest intelligence along with profiteering intelligence, at the same time that it implies the confusion of mind which is likely to lead to still more false intellectualism, is dangerous in another way; for it brings into contempt the science and art of the use of words. Practical men in a practical time are naturally disposed to turn upon men of words and to revenge themselves for their habitual subordination by contrasting their present indispensability with the assumed superfluousness of mere men of letters. But not only will this mood pass, but it rests upon assumptions which could only be true if men were nothing more than accomplished animals. I respect the engineer and the ship-builder—every good workman of one trade respects the good workmen of every other trade—but, at the end of it all, what more is an engineer than a marvellous beaver? To discover, not more and more things, but more and more the truth or the real relations of things, is, on the other hand, what distinguishes men from animals. Man, in short, is the truth-seeking creature; and any material function, however ingeniously discharged, is properly subordinate to this, his unique research. But words are the tools of this trade. Words are to truth what raw materials are to any industry—the substance upon which, and with which, the directing mind must work. True enough that they are most readily susceptible of error, and that few minds can deal with them with precision. But the effort must not be given up on that account. Rather, indeed, it behoves us to be a thousand times more critical. And, again, it is not as if we can ever dispense with words, good, bad, or indifferent. A democracy is governed by words; all human government, in fact, is logocracy. To the extent, therefore, that the use of words is properly understood, government, even in the most practical affairs, is itself good. What, for instance, have practical men not had to pay for the failure of our intelligentsia to impress upon the public the distinction between Equality and Identity, Liberty and Doing as One Pleases, Impartiality and Neutrality? To belittle the right use of words, with the results of their wrong use before our eyes, is to invite still worse practical confusion. The only cure for intellectual dishonesty is intellectual honesty.

MINISTERING TO A STYLE DISEASED

A letter from a friend charges me with a strong tendency to subject the æsthetic to the ethical in my criticisms of literature. The accusation irks me a little, for I must have given so fair a critic an excuse for it. Let me then explain myself. The first ground that could conceivably be taken against me is that I subordinate my valuation of a man's work to my valuation of his personal character—after the manner of the Puritans, who deny that good can come out of Galilee. But the very reverse of this is actually my case, for I contend that a man's character is revealed in his work as it is not, and cannot be, in his mere life. ('As for living,' said Villiers de l'Isle Adam for every artist, 'our servants can do that for us.') Do not tell me, I have often said to biographers, what porridge had John Keats or what earthly experiences befell Shelley. Only in so far as these things show in style are they of any possible value; and, without knowing them otherwise at all, the critic can divine as much of them as he needs. The style is the man; and his works are his life—all his life, at least, that concerns the literary critic. Next, it might be assumed that I import moral decadence as exhibited in personal character into literature and find there what I presumably look for. But it is not so. Any moral decadence, so-called, that conceals itself from the eye of the critic of pure literature is to my mind irrelevant to criticism. Either it is discoverable in the style or it is not; and if not, what have I, as a critic, to do with it? I do, however, contend, that moral decadence may be discovered in style itself. It is shown in the very construction of a man's sentences, in his rhythm, in his syntax. That a man who writes badly has the seeds of bad conduct in him I firmly believe; but *qua* critic, it is his bad writing I complain of, and not its after or before illustrations in his conduct. Lastly, I imagine it may be held that my condemnation of certain writers' choice of subject is itself proof of a moral bias in æsthetic matters. But, here again, my criterion is purely literary. Theoretically, every subject is open to every writer; but, practically, every good writer chooses the subject that best suits his powers. Because there is admittedly a hierarchy of subjects, must I not place in the highest rank the writers whose choice of subject is elevated, and who write up to it; and in a lower rank the writers who choose petty subjects even when they write up to these? And the consciousness of power that impels a man to the former choice is evidence at the same time of his wholeness; as the consciousness of only a little power that leads to the lower choice is also evidence of a writer's failure in wholeness— in short, of his decadence. Decadence is at once a moral and an æsthetic term; but decadence, for me as a critic, is absence of a mission, of a purpose, of a co-ordination of powers; and its sign manual in style is the diffuse sentence, the partial treatment, the inchoate vocabulary, the mixed principles. When I have discovered these I would, it is true, hand the writer over to a critic to be cured—but only of bad style of mind. Ministering to a style diseased is one of the peculiar tasks of the critic.

THE STYLE IS THE MAN

In his popular edition of *Self-selected Essays*, Mr. Augustine Birrell puts a postscript to his essay on Edmund Burke: 'When I wrote this I had read Burke, but not a great deal about him; and the more you read Burke in his *Collected Works* the greater becomes your admiration; but the more you read about him . . . the harder it is to like him as much as I at least desire to do.' This footnote shows what comes of reading too much of a man's private life, of listening to a great man's valet. But it reveals much more, namely, the heresy upon which I am always willing to fling my faggot, of contrasting a man's life and his work. Observe what Mr. Birrell permits himself to be guilty of contending: that whereas the more he reads of Burke the more he admires him, the more he reads about him the less he likes him. Setting aside the manifest absurdity of contrasting admiration with liking or of expecting to like what one admires—the clash of judgement involved in a simultaneous increase of admiration for Burke's Works, and decrease of admiration for Burke himself, argues a defect of judgement in one or other respect, if not in both. Either Mr. Birrell is less critical of Burke's Works than he ought to be, or he is too critical of Burke's personal character; for what is much more credible than that character and Works are contrasted—to admit which would simply disestablish every principle of moral judgement in æsthetics and leave æsthetics without a friend in the nature of man—is that Mr. Birrell is wrong in one or other respect.

Having myself lately read the most scandalous accounts of Burke that have been published, I am quite prepared to agree with Mr. Birrell that the more you hear of Burke the less you are disposed to like him. But even as to this, there is the distinction to be remembered that to hear of and to experience a person are by no means the same thing. On merely hearing reports of what a man has actually done, or is in the habit of doing, you may come to the conclusion (if you are very inexperienced) that on meeting the man himself you will inevitably feel towards him exactly as you feel towards those reports. Nothing, however, turns out more commonly different. Often and often we come away charmed from the meeting with a man of whom we have before heard nothing but evil, and vice versa. May it not have been the same with Burke? Would Mr. Birrell have disliked him so much if, instead of only hearing about him, he had met him, even in the very circumstances of which the reports speak? But this, you may say, is to introduce the personal equation into an act of judgement; and to allow the mind to be seduced into a rosy judgement by reason of the judge's partiality. Let it be so—though, in truth, there is more sense in the remark that one ought to speak of men as one finds them, rather than as others find them. Let it be the case that Mr. Birrell is right in concluding to like Burke less the more he hears of him—the difficulty will then remain to explain why he admires Burke's Works the more he reads them. My impression is that Mr. Birrell must be compensating himself for frustrated liking of the man by an access of admiration for his Works. Determined to make an idol of Burke, he worships the more vigorously the golden head on beholding more clearly the feet of clay; but at the cost of blindness, wilful even if unconscious. What am I saying? Only that as many as were the defects of character in Burke himself, so many and no fewer or smaller were the defects in Burke's Works; and that Mr. Birrell should see them. He has not fallen into the vulgar error of reading into a man's work the defects he has discovered, by reading *about* him, in his character; but he has fallen into the opposite error of discovering in the work no trace of the defects of character, as if Burke and his work were different beings. But they are the same. Burke the writer and Burke the man are not two different persons, of whom the one the more you know the more you must admire him, and the other the more the less. Literary criticism, on the other hand, is concerned as wholly with Burke as personal criticism is; and with only this difference, that whereas personal criticism takes account of men's relations with persons—its material being conduct in general—literary criticism passes judgement on a man as revealed in the material of his work. There is thus no contrast to be made between Burke the writer of the *Collected Works* and Burke the subject of the Memoirs. In so far as the criticisms of each of the two aspects of Burke—his literary and his personal—are complete, they must needs coincide. The literary judgement must agree with the personal and the personal with the literary; they cannot both analyse the same man and come to contrary conclusions.

It is clear that Mr. Birrell has failed to examine Burke the writer with anything like the seriousness with which he has examined him as a man. Shall I be accused of arriving at a foregone result if I say that I expected to come to it? Mr. Birrell is a man of *esprit*, a delightful writer; he has gaiety, charm, wit, and a proper degree of sentiment. But he is, at bottom, the cultured Philistine. Matthew Arnold, after all, has not left the Philistines without a witness of his

influence upon them. Since his day they have taken themselves in hand with the thoroughness he attributed to them,
reading this and that—poetry and works of imagination,
as well as history and philosophy—going here and there,
and generally cultivating receptivity with commendable
industry. But they remain Philistines still—minds essentially
unimpressionable to the great, the tragic, the sublime, the
elevated. Here is Mr. Birrell, for instance, the pupil of
Arnold, the fruit of his culture; on his own confession one
of the 'decent sober-minded folk who love virtue, and, on
the whole, *prefer* delicate humour to sickly lubricity'. Very
modest, you see, but only *preferring* one thing to its opposite;
yet claiming to 'love' virtue. Is it not obvious throughout
all his essays that Mr. Birrell does not love any more than
he hates: that he has only preferences, likes or dislikes,
hobbies, as it were, but never pursuits and passions? This
coldness, while it enables Mr. Birrell to be one of the wittiest,
most readable and sensible essayists in English, not only
excludes him from the history of English literature, wherein
he will never figure as more than a taster, but puts beyond his
comprehension the grand qualities of a writer like Burke,
and hence Burke's grand defects. For Burke, despite all his
personal littleness, had a grand side to his character—which
Johnson, for example, realized and admired; he had also,
because of those defects, a mean side to his work. Put
Burke's personal life aside: forget that you ever learned
anything about him as a man; and judge him as he revealed
himself in his work—is it the fact that one must admire him
the more one reads him? I think of his petty meanness in
the indictment he drew up of the tremendous figure of
Warren Hastings—a political attorney prosecuting a hero
of tragedy with never a suspicion of the magnitude of the
tragedy. I think of his failure to divine the tragical meaning
of the French Revolution. I think of the pomposity of his
style whenever he approaches an aspect of the sublime.

C

These were the grand defects of Burke; and they are to be read in his style, even when we choose to remain ignorant of his life. Such as were his Works such was his life; not different, but the same. Mr. Birrell, who sees nothing grand in Burke's life, sees nothing small in his work. But the great and the small are in both.

ONE READER'S NOTEBOOK

Samuel Butler remarked on several occasions (as if it were an ever-present reflection with him) that a born literary man is to be known by his carrying of a small notebook in his upper waistcoat pocket. I have never carried a notebook in my waistcoat pocket, though I read of it in Butler long enough ago to adopt the evidence of vocation before my friends could suspect me of fraud. But on the other hand, I have always carried a substantial notebook in my side pocket for extracts and reflections picked up in divers places and in sundry fashions. Of all that I have filled, however, I do not now possess a single one: they have been destroyed by my own hand. And the reason is this: So soon as one is filled (and it takes about a year to ripen it) I sift it with a fine sieve and copy out into a large manuscript book everything I either cannot remember or am afraid I may forget. This home-staying volume is by this time fairly well-to-do in personal treasure. Not so full as you would suppose, however, after having received the harvest of a dozen to a score respectably sized pocketbooks. For the fact is that I have, I find, no use for long extracts; and the very longest in my collection is not more than about forty words, counting the particles in. I do not always distinguish the author, either, I find; so that you may sometimes be blaming me for phrases that belong to somebody else. On the other hand, I must often be turning the cat in the pan (as the

saying is) by attributing to a third person little jewels of
my own.

The occasion of the foregoing thrilling personal revelation is the destruction from which I have just come of
my latest notebook. Begun, I see, in January, it has over-
stayed its year in my pocket by some months; and now that
I have winnowed its contents, I think its year must have
been comparatively unfruitful: a single page of my thesaurus
is all that it has yielded. However, I do not complain. There
was so much the less to copy out. And perhaps it is the case
that my taste is becoming more fastidious: I am harde₋ to
be persuaded to make a permanent note of it. But is that
so indeed? I turn over the leaves of my mausoleum and
compare year's yield with year's yield. No. I do not seem
to be more exigent than before. How discerning, on the
contrary, I appear to have always been! (I mean nothing
flattering to myself, gentle reader, but only that what
delighted me ten years ago delights me still.) Then to what
is due the poverty of the past year? I will give up the question:
it is of no account whatever.

You will expect after this that I should now set down
here at any rate a selection from my final selection. At the
cost of making a third copy I shall oblige you. (No, no, not
at all, the pleasure is mine!) Let me begin, then, with a
sample of happy adjectives, as I may call them: adjectives,
that is, surprisingly suited to their substantives. Here are
two, and I know, though I shall not tell, where they came
from: 'Belloc's *burly* judgement'; 'a *needy* knock at the
door'. Well? Oh, but you must not think that such marriages
are easy to arrange: the path of true writing never did run
smooth. Try it. I must have read or heard some dialect and
technical phrases suitable to be used in writing; for here
are several worth my noting. That turning of the cat in the
pan, for instance, is a recent conquest. I never used it before

in my life. And here is a phrase you may look to find early
and often: 'Working under forced draught'. You, of course,
have heard it before, and so have I; but never have I realized
its uses fully until now. Here is a proverb fairly happily
mixed, I think, and applicable, I should say, to one who
troubles trouble before trouble troubles him: 'Don't count
your chickens before they come home to roost'. You may
have that and call it your own if you like, for the author
will never claim it. Here is a sentence that Jeremy Taylor
thought worth quoting without mentioning the author's
name. It was to serve me for a story one day; but I am
reckless, and it shall go down here: 'She that is loved is
safe; and he that loves is joyful'. What a young world that
calls up, and we this side of Eden!

On a cognate subject I find the following sentence: 'A
cultured country is one in which even the most sensitive
woman is not sorry to have been born a woman'. The sentence bears no name, and for the simple reason that nobody
wrote it. If it were better than it is, I should have said, as
Blake used to say, that its author is in eternity; meaning,
I take it, that the sentence was inspired. As a matter of fact,
I found it complete in my mind one morning without
having been aware of constructing it. And that reminds me.
Years ago, crossing the fields on a visit to a friend living
in a detached suburb, I was suddenly seized and brought to
a full stop by a sentence that insisted on saying itself to me.
It was this: 'And they shall beat their sorrows into song, and
their mirth into instruments of music'. Now, where did
that come from? I have never met it anywhere to my knowledge, save in those fields. A letter of thanks shall be the
reward of anybody who discovers me the author of it. 'To
talk about things that interest everybody in language that
everybody understands'—this, I imagine, I wrote myself
while reflecting upon some books upon Style. It defines

the minimum of good writing, but we are not taken over scratch by it: the course remains to be run. 'Not living but lingering'—that is only so-so. It has no name, and I do not own it. But here's a better: 'Leaving a fountain to run to a puddle'. I am rather taken by that. But, again, it is bettered by this: 'You know the thorns, I see the rose'. Capitalized, the phrase appears to blossom almost into poetry: 'You know the Thorns, I see the Rose'. Who that has an intimate knowledge of persons or circumstances of a forbidding exterior has not at times had the thought in mind? The Crown of Thorns; the Crown of Roses!

The following are without a name, but I should not call them inspired: 'Laws of Nature are the Tables of Affinity between Phenomena'. I could have said that myself; and possibly I shall one of these days. 'To make the body more and more the servant of the brain, and the brain more and more the servant of the heart.' That, too, is somewhat pedestrian, if not actually mechanical. The repetition of 'more and more' and the geometrical symmetry of the sentence's parts are incompatible with originality. The sentence was made, not born. 'Women are being driven from a vocation into an occupation.' Everything here is of dubious value; I have little use for it. The following is better, however: 'War is like Life, you never know whether you like it or not'; I can imagine the phrase becoming as classic as the sergeant-major's remark in the midst of the trenches: 'It would never do to take this war seriously'. The expression is sublime in its relevant irrelevance. And what do you think of this for a fancy: 'Only let the band go down the streets of Heaven, and every soul will follow it to earth'? Too fanciful, you say. Very well, but it rather pleases one who has a fondness for the doctrine of Reincarnation, *and* sometimes wonders why people are born. In the same vein is this that 'we have taken on flesh, but the

less said about it the better'. Perhaps we have here a clue
to the feeling of repulsion some of us have to physiological
realism in its various forms. For my part, I swear I am not
a Puritan in the ordinary sense of the word. The ordinary
moral shock of the bourgeois is a sensation unknown to me.
And yet I derive no pleasure from the treatment in literature
or art of crude physiology. Why such a fuss about an accident, I ask? Yes, yes, curious, and interesting; of course,
of course, *very* important! Ah, really! But excuse my
yawns—shall we resume our conversation about the mind?

THE PERFECTIBILITY OF ENGLISH

In the midst of his trivial relations of his trivial observations
among trivial people, Mr. George Moore makes one remark
the discussion of which might be useful. 'The source', he
says, 'from which language is refreshed—rural English—is
being destroyed by Council Schools; and God help the
writer who puts pen to paper in fifty years' time.' I do not
agree with either of the implied propositions, but I do not
deny that there is something to be said for them. The
sources of literature in the dialect are indeed in danger of
drying up, if they are not dried up already; the great
'Dialect Dictionary' has, in fact, as good as reported on the
post-mortem of local variations. But on the other hand,
the colloquial is always with us and offers the prospect of a
boundless reciprocity with literary language. Admitting
for the sake of the argument that literary language is the
synthesis of dialects, its perfection is only possible when these
have been assimilated and in their turn restored to common
colloquial currency. Literature, so to say, takes up dialect
and, after using it, restores it to speech in a purified and
universal instead of local form. Thus the perfection of Greek
was to be found, I should say, in Plato and Demosthenes,

two of the simplest and most colloquial writers that ever
lived. Swift in English is often indistinguishable from careful
conversation; and, generally, style becomes perfect as it
becomes natural—that is, colloquial. Thus the future of the
writer is not the gloomy one foreseen by Mr. George
Moore, for there can scarcely be an end to the perfectibility
of language in simplicity. It is, on the contrary, a future of
infinite attraction. Only when some writer arises as simple
and yet as profound as Plato, or as simple and yet as im-
passioned as Demosthenes, shall I begin to feel any appre-
hension of the approaching surcease of literary progress.

PURIFIED TALK

Cobbett does not deserve what Green says of him, that he
was 'the greatest tribune the English poor ever possessed'.
Cobbett had not sufficient appreciation of the real enemy
of the English poor, and it is safe to say of his projects of
reform, as of so many others, that if they could all have been
carried, the English poor would have remained the English
poor. A much more lasting effect and testimony to his
tribuneship is to be found in his style, which is as near an
approach to good spoken English as any writer is ever
likely to make. Not to English as spoken by the educated
classes; still less to English as spoken by the uneducated. It
has neither class distinction nor distinction of dialect; but
it is what we call plain English. Mark how closely his
sentences follow speech in both vocabulary and construction:

The farmers here, as everywhere else, complain most bitterly;
but they hang on, like sailors to the masts or hull of a wreck.

It [the land system] is staggering about like a sheep with water
in the head, turning its pate up on one side, seeming to listen, but
it has no hearing; seeming to look, but it has no sight; one day it
capers and dances; the next it mopes and seems ready to die.

Old dread-death and dread-devil Johnson, that teacher of moping and melancholy! If the writings of this time-serving, mean, dastardly old pensioner had got a firm hold of the minds of the people at large, the people would have been bereft of their very souls.

The qualities of such writing are hard to define for the very reason that they are so well concealed. There is no appearance of art; and I should fancy that Cobbett never saw the end of the sentence in writing, as we do not in speech, before beginning it. It is writ straight on as we talk straight on. But anybody who thinks it easy to imitate on that account will discover his mistake upon trial. Cobbett's style was Cobbett. On the other hand, it would be to fall into no less a mistake to suppose that the acquirement of his style was never any effort to Cobbett himself. We are told that while in the army he read and got by heart an English grammar, which he used to repeat while doing sentry. We know also that he wrote one of the best English grammars even now in existence. His simplicity, though natural, had to be maintained and developed. For it is just the natural and the simple that needs the greatest art.

THE SUBLIME LONGINUS

Who the author of the famous essay was, and when his work first appeared, are matters still in dispute. But what is not in dispute is that whoever the author was he was one of the greatest of critical geniuses, and that whenever he wrote, it was in an age when criticism was pursued as a fine art. Each of the conclusions is established for a good judge in the course of the reading of the essay itself; for, in the first place, over and over again we come across

observations of such insight and illumination that we cannot
doubt we are reading the work of a master; and, as for the
second conclusion, it cannot be otherwise than that a man
thus writing at the altitude and with the sureness of Longinus
found himself in the midst of an age when criticism was a
common, and, so to say, a fashionable, pursuit. It is true
that Longinus, very much as one of ourselves might do,
complains a little of the times upon which he had fallen.
But let us note and envy the nature of his complaint; it is
that all his contemporaries were seeking novelities of style,
expression, phrasing, and the rest. But is not that to say that
literary criticism was a kind of craze, as I wish to Longinus
it were with us; and hence that Longinus was really in
a great current, though, to be sure, he preached, as we
might preach, Back to the Classics, to a world esurient for
novelty?

The price we must pay for the absence of criticism is
monotony of production; and, surely enough, we are paying
it. Contemporary writing has many good qualities, and
never, indeed, was there a time when so many people could
write so tolerably well as nowadays. But contemporary
prose has no excellencies, no elevation, no real distinction.
For us, therefore, above all ages that ever were, *Longinus on
the Sublime* is the very critic we need; for to no other end
than the appreciation and the creation of the elevated, the
excellent and the sublime, was his essay directed. (It is
curious, by the way, to observe that the common explanation
in Longinus' day of the flatness of the contemporary prose
was precisely *not* democracy. Longinus wrote under an
Empire, and during a period of profound peace; and he set
himself to combat the popular notion that the democracy
for which his contemporaries sighed—just as, on the other
hand, our would-be critics sigh against democracy—was
necessary to great art. Neither democracy nor oligarchy

he concludes, is more or less favourable to literature: it is plutocracy that is fatal, and plutocracy is compatible with any form of government.)

In what does elevation or real eloquence consist; and how is it to be observed? Longinus replies that the sublime is the outcome of two things: good fortune, or a natural endowment of sensibility, and good counsel or art, and that it is to be distinguished by its effect of producing 'transport' (Professor Roberts' translation) or 'ecstasy', as I should prefer to call it. Modern prose has as its sole aim persuasion by means of dialectic; it addresses itself to the reason, and to this end confines its employment of material mainly to the useful or the necessary. But the useful and the necessary, says Longinus, men naturally regard as commonplace; and it therefore follows that the prose that deals exclusively with them is commonplace likewise. Moreover, persuasion by dialectic is not only resistible, but what is done by its means can be undone by the same means. Persuasion, in short, is precarious. The 'sublime', on the other hand, does not persuade; it overpowers, seizes, and holds captive; it is irresistible, and its effects are permanent; for what is admired has more and more lasting influence than what is only reasonable. But how to create the sublime—there's the rub. Assuming the natural endowment of extreme sensibility ('sublimity is the echo of a great soul'), Longinus then proceeds to discuss the literary art of sublime expression, taking his examples mainly from the Greek classics. To these he adds the admonition that such examples must be read many times, and deliberately studied with a view to emulating them. It is no use, he says, pursuing the literary art in a 'half-hearted' way, as if an occasional dip into a model and an occasional exercise in deliberate writing were sure, in the end, to result in a grand style. We must write as if Homer and Demosthenes were to be our judges; and as if our lives depended upon their approval. But can we, in these days, find a sufficient motive for this whole-hearted devotion? All perfection is the fruit of sacrifice, and there appears to be nothing nowadays worth the sacrifice involved in the perfection of the art of writing.

One or two remarks made by Longinus in passing are worth remembering for life. Here is one that gives me a peculiar satisfaction, since I re-discovered it for myself: 'The judgement of style is the last and crowning fruit of long experience'. Henceforth Longinus shall be my authority. Here is another with which, praise be to our good fortune, we are likewise familiar, though in forms less neat: 'Art is perfect when it seems to be nature'. Is not that itself an illustration? The following observation bears closely upon contemporary literary criticism. Why, asks Longinus, cannot good judgement be bought? Because, he replies, judgement that can be bought cannot be good. I have elsewhere referred to Mr. Shaw's recent defence of mixed metaphors under any circumstances—for Mr. Shaw did not discriminate their times and seasons. Mixed metaphors, says Longinus, are only justified when they are the expression of passion. In other moods, their appearance is offensive.

THE DANGER OF THE WHIMSICAL

Lamb holds a high place in English literature, and deserves to be challenged as well as saluted every decade or so. His style owes its characteristics to Burton and Sterne, each of whom contributed a recognizable feature. Much reading of Burton gave Lamb the taste for out-of-the-way words; much reading of Sterne liquefied his sentences so that they ran in and out, with parenthetical eddies upon them, like a stream in flood. His ideas, however, have been sacrificed to the charm which the dilettantes have discovered in his style. Actually Lamb is a greater critic than his present reputation gives him credit for. The essays upon 'The Sanity of True Genius' and 'The Genius and Character of Hogarth', for example, are, as criticism, equal to Hazlitt, Coleridge, and De Quincey at their best. But why has this *strength* of Lamb been forgotten? In part, because every age reduces its predecessors to its own compass; and emphatically good criticism is not popular to-day. But in part it is due to Lamb himself. With a sincere and severe taste in art and literature, he could seldom avoid playing monkey-tricks in his expression of it. The whimsical overcame his natural good judgement, and he succumbed as easily to a facetious triviality in the midst of a serious essay as to a pun in the midst of a serious conversation. It is all very well to say that this very whimsicality constitutes part of his charm. For such as think so, the critic Lamb scarcely exists. They dangle round him—as, no doubt, some of his fellow-clerks did—for his witticisms, while feeling only bored by his genuine ideas. Others, of whom I am one, find no charm in the fancy of 'a mermaid over a fish-kettle cooking her own tail'. Lamb found it 'irresistibly' funny, and so probably do his lesser admirers. But Lear and Lewis Carroll could do it much better; and in Lamb such fancies are as incongruous as Thackeray setting up to be a draughtsman.

Since he could not help saying that he preferred babies 'b-b-boiled', or writing upon 'Roast Pig', he should have attributed this impish part of his mind to an inviolate pseudonym and reserved his proper name for his critical essays. These latter have suffered from the company they keep, and will continue to do so until they are published separately. A judge of literature cannot afford to indulge in witticisms.

Lamb is at his best as a critic in his essay upon Garrick.

Struck, as we all must have been, by the banality of the association of Garrick with Shakespeare upon Garrick's tomb in Westminster Abbey—'Shakespeare and Garrick, like twin-stars, shall shine'—Lamb set himself to expressing what we all feel, the real inequality of the arts of acting and writing. Nobody seriously considers the actor the equal of the writer; and it was probably only upon a wave of journalistic emotion that Garrick got into the Abbey at all. As well honour the executant of Beethoven with Beethoven himself, as Garrick with Shakespeare. The one was for a few nights, the other is for all time. Lamb goes further, however, than to dissociate the two in value. He would dissociate them altogether. Though he was tolerant of acting, he much preferred the reading to the hearing of a great play. How much more subtly one can read a play of Shakespeare than anybody can speak it, or, still less, act it. A thousand inflexions are made in the mind that cannot be conveyed either by voice or by gesture. Voice and gesture at best must make a selection from the meanings the writer conveyed; they are one interpretation only. And at their worst they do no more than adapt—which is to say distort—the play to the popular mind. A popular representation of a great play is usually a misrepresentation.

A SELF-MADE CRITIC: WATTS-DUNTON

In a spirit of gratitude, if not of judgement, Swinburne called Theodore Watts-Dunton the greatest critic of poetry of his generation. Swinburne, however, was never a judge, but always a brilliant advocate; and Watts-Dunton was his solicitor. The famous article on Poetry which the latter contributed to the *Encyclopædia Britannica* has been reprinted. What could have attracted our predecessors so greatly to this essay? It is not only painstakingly dull, but it is wrong upon matters in which to be wrong is almost a crime. The author says, for instance, that Matthew Arnold's remark that poetry is a criticism of life meant that Arnold demanded of poetry 'generalizations on human life'. But you have only to turn to Arnold's own illustrations of poetry to see that nothing in the way of reflections or generalizations about life was in his mind. When he quotes as an example of pure poetry Wordsworth's line: 'And never lifted up a single stone', or Shakespeare's lines about the daffodils, where was any generalization about human life in it? Watts-Dunton completely misunderstood Arnold's phrase; and the misunderstanding revealed the fundamental defects of a critic not born but painfully made. Look, too, at the style in which Watts-Dunton wrote of poetry: the training of the solicitor is over it all. 'Assuredly no philosophy of history can be other than inadequate should it ignore the fact that poetry has had as much effect upon human destiny as that other great human energy by aid of which, from the discovery of the use of fire to that of the electric light, the useful arts have been developed.' It is a plea and a defence for poetry, supported by legal evidence that poetry is a utility comparable with the utility of science! But the two are not to be compared in this way; for the 'use' of poetry is precisely in contrast, and not in comparison with the 'use' of science. Relatively to the utility of science the distinction of poetry is that it is useless: its aim is in itself and not as a means to anything else. We can, however, gather from Watts-Dunton's attitude the explanation of his appeal to his generation. His was one of the earliest challenges to the Victorian tyranny of Science. And he grew bolder, it must be said, as the years passed by and the criticism of poetry once more came into fashion. The difference between his early essay on 'Poetry' and his later essay on the 'Renascence of Wonder' is considerable. In the latter he is no longer apologetic for poetry in the presence of Science, but a little contemptuous of Science. I do not attach any importance, of course, either to the phrase or to the idea of a 'Renascence of Wonder'. It is not criticism but journalism. At the same time it comes near to treating poetry on its merits as poetry rather than as a rival of Science.

Watts-Dunton's remark may be noted that 'absolute poetry is the concrete and artistic expression of the human mind in emotional and rhythmical language'. Compare this with a definition given by Mr. Stephen Coleridge. 'Poetry', says Mr. Coleridge, 'is the highest expression that man has found for the deepest emotions of his heart.' And even this leaves, it must be said, a great deal to be filled-in—for the question is unanswered what form this 'highest expression' takes. Is it of necessity rhythmical; or can it be any form? Mr. Coleridge's own opinion, elsewhere expressed than in his definition, is that it must be rhythmical, for he turns out Whitman from among the poets with considerable harshness; and with no more ceremony he evicts Mr. John Masefield for using bad language.

STEVENSON AND THE ART OF PROSE

Stevenson's *Art of Writing* contains, along with a number of surprising misunderstandings, one or two fragmentary observations fit for the final treatise on style of my imagination. For instance, upon style in its craft-aspect, Stevenson said what in my judgement is both original and true, namely, that it is the one essential quality of writing in which deliberate self-improvement is always possible. Other essential qualities of writing are, as it were, gifts of nature and experience; but the perfection of a personal style is a work of art, or, if I may play on the phrase, the art of work. With this criterion we ought to be able to apply a scientific stylometry to literature in general, and to classify periods both in respect of schools and individuals with the accuracy of connoisseurs.

Stevenson had a false modesty upon the subject of literary analysis which did his admirable curiosity no honour. Even while he was engaged in it, and enjoying the exercise thoroughly, he pretended to feel like a vandal pulling a rose to pieces to discover the secret of its beauty. The experiment is comparable to nothing of the kind, nor is it even comparable to another pastime to which Stevenson likened it, that of a child pulling a musical-box to pieces. In these cases the rose and the box are destroyed in the process; but in the former case the wonder and the beauty of literature remain, and are, in fact, enhanced in our realization of them by the very process of analysis, or pulling literature to pieces. If it were, indeed, the fact that after a careful analysis a poem or an essay ceased to be beautiful for us, richly would our analysis have rewarded us; for the refinement of our sense of beauty is essential to the appreciation of excelling work. But upon many occasions in English literature—praise be to famous men—the more you analyse it, the more mysteriously beautiful it becomes.

The process is rather like anatomizing the body in fear of destroying the soul, but only to discover that the soul is thereby isolated beyond us. As all that can be anatomized is precisely not life, so all that can be analysed is precisely not literature; for literature stands to writing as life stands to body. Let us analyse away, then, as hard as we please, and with a good conscience. We shall discover many secrets by its means, but we shall never destroy, but only isolate, the mystery of literature.

In his account of the nature of prose, Stevenson failed to be anything more than negative. His only conception of the rhythm of prose was that it should not be the rhythm of verse. 'It may be anything,' he says, 'but it must not be verse.' Curiously enough, upon the very page upon which

Stevenson says this of prose, he himself falls into blank
verse unconsciously:

> but for that very reason word is linked
> suggest no measure but the one in hand
> one following another will produce.

And on turning over the same prose essay we find him
lapsing into blank verse on at least another score of occasions.
So much for precept and example. But Stevenson was surely
wrong in regarding prose as merely not-verse; and, again,
when he says that 'the rule of rhythm in prose is not so
intricate as the rule in verse'. It is not regular, of course;
and it is, therefore, not so obvious. In fact, Stevenson was
right when he said that the rhythm of prose should never
be as obvious as the rhythm of verse. But that it is less intricate on this account is the very reverse of the truth; it is far
more intricate. I am perhaps a little jealous for the fair fame
of prose. I resent the insinuation of the verse-makers that
verse is more difficult, more honourable, or more beautiful
than prose. A perfect prose is the last word in literature,
since it contains every kind of rhythm to be found in verse,
and other rhythms as well, and all in such a rich variety and
seeming irregularity that while no rhythm is insistent every
rhythm is heard. Verse is a solo, a melody; it is, if you like,
something even more elaborate, a harmony of chords, a
sonata, a composition for the organ; but it is always played
upon a single instrument. Prose is an orchestra, consisting
not only of all the instruments on which verse can be
played, but of instruments unanswerable to verse. Where
in verse will you find the foot of more than, at the most,
four syllables? And even these quadrupeds (the antispast,
choriamb, di-iamb, dispondee, etc.) can rarely be made to
dance in a measure. But in prose, not only have we the use
of the two-, the three-, and the four-syllabled feet, but the
five- (the dochmiac) and the six-syllabled as well. The craft

D

of prose is the employment of these rhythms without the appearance of rhythm. Their very variety makes it possible to disguise their individual existence. They mix and mingle in such rapid succession that the reader can never be aware of one more than of another. It is the charm of the rhythm of prose that it steals upon the senses without detection. To say, therefore, that the rhythm of prose is less intricate than the rhythm of verse is the triumph of prose over criticism. Prose laughs at Stevenson while he says it; and, in revenge, trips him up with his blank lines to prove how much more easily verse may be written than prose. I wish Stevenson were alive to hear what prose thinks of him. He was an honest craftsman, and I think he would have enjoyed being corrected for his improvement.

MR. 'JACOB TONSON': THE END IN VIEW

Mr. Bennett ('Jacob Tonson') has many of the right prejudices for a polemical literary critic desirous of 'helping the sacred cause'—to use his own phrase. He was the first critic to apply the withering word 'mandarins' to the academic anatomists of literature—the Professors Saintsbury, Raleigh, Churton Collins, Herford, etc. His complaint of them is the natural complaint of the skilled craftsman, that they are not themselves skilled in the craft they profess to judge. For the same reason he condemns Literary Academies in this country: they would be sure to be composed (and the event has proved it) of mandarins, accomplished or predestined. He was an apostle, too, of freedom in writing, both as to subject and style. There is always something new to be said, and always fresh, effective ways of saying it; and no tradition, he urges, should be allowed to stand in the way of discovering them. Such a wholesale invitation to all and sundry to experiment is full

of dangers—as, indeed, has been proved by the literary
wrecks that strew our libraries; and equally, I think, no
great writer would ever dream of following such advice;
for to the extent that a writer knows himself to be original
he usually elects to work within the great traditions of his
craft. But it was advice distinctly encouraging to young
writers. It encouraged them to 'be themselves', to strike
and to write—even when they could not. Nobody knows
how many writers Mr. Bennett has made whom God never
intended to write at all. And for this he deserves, and, I
believe, has received, their gratitude, if not ours, in one
form or another.

Let that pass as praise, and let me now turn to the other
side of the picture. I have said that Mr. Bennett's outlook is
restricted by rationalism; and this is manifested by, amongst
other things, his preference for Mr. Lucas over Mr. G. K.
Chesterton on the ground that Mr. Chesterton cannot
have 'a first-class intellectual apparatus', since he accepts
dogma.

'It is impossible', says Mr. Bennett, 'for a young man of
first-class intellect to accept any form of dogma.' But how
faded does that dogma of rationalism now appear in the
light even of modern ethical speculation, to say nothing of
Plato. Rationalism itself is only one of the minor dogmas
of a universe whose very foundations are dogmatic. Mr.
Bennett's rationalism, moreover, is of a lower variety than
that of the classical rationalists; it approximates when it does
not reach to materialism itself. This is evident in the absence
from Mr. Bennett's critical apparatus of any appreciation
of art as distinct from craft. I have praised Mr. Bennett's
praise and practice of good workmanship: without good
workmanship there is no art worth consideration. But in
Mr. Bennett's mind good workmanship and good art are
convertible terms. Coleridge it was who said that when he

spoke of ideas, his hearers thought of bricks and mortar; and I should say that when Mr. Bennett is writing of art he is thinking of craft. His preoccupation with the craft of writing is exclusive. Everything connected with it, including its wages, is a matter of absorbing interest to him. He is never weary of discussing the craft structure of literary work from its inception to its sale and effect upon the public. And he will use himself as an illustration without any modesty whatever. By the time you have read all that he has written on the subject of authorship, you know his own hours and methods and motives and remunerations of work as if you were a fellow craftsman in the same shop with him. He is very generous of himself in this respect. But what all the while one misses is a recognition that the artist is something more than a craftsman, or is concerned with other matters than the technique of turning out good and saleable stuff. Good and saleable, be it observed; for the one, we must observe, is as indispensable in Mr. Bennett's opinion as the other. To be saleable, to sell, to make a great deal of money by it, is not the only ambition or criterion of the work set up by Mr. Bennett; the work itself must be good, and this in his opinion literally means work and nothing more. His gospel amounts to this: that anybody can succeed as a writer who puts his back into it as if it were a business, and is willing to make and sell good stuff. But need I say that this is not the whole truth? Nor is it in the least true that the preoccupation of the artist is with the craft, or with anything connected with it. Occupation in the craft is, of course, a necessity of the artist, but his preoccupation is with something altogether different, namely, with what he has to say and the effect he intends to produce. This distinction between the artist-craftsman and the craftsman is precisely in this matter of preoccupation. While the latter thinks of nothing so much as how he shall say it, the former thinks of nothing so much as what he shall say. The artist-craftsman is primarily a thinker, a teacher, a seer, a missionary; the craftsman wants to make a future and a reputation.

But Mr. Bennett is so far from understanding the psychology of the artist that he imagines him to be exhausted in the psychology of the craftsman; and in contradiction of well-known facts (including those of his own personal experience) he asserts that all 'authors capable of producing really high-class stuff . . . are strangely keen on getting the best possible remuneration for it'. Never you believe, he says, that genuine artists are indifferent to money. I should not like to say that every genuine artist has been indifferent to money; I would not deny offhand that some authors capable of producing high-class stuff have been keen on getting well paid for it; but it is not the rule, it is not the tradition; and I am not certain that it is the fact. English literature would be very poor if it had to depend upon writers strangely keen on getting paid top-prices, or even upon getting any remuneration whatever. The sums actually spent upon literature in any country have never afforded an income for some of its greatest writers, whose motive to keep on must, therefore, have been something other than money.

A LESSON IN PROSE TECHNIQUE

I indulge myself in the luxury of a particular analysis. The following passage is taken from De Quincey's *Suspiria*—from De Quincey, who, more deliberately than any other writer in English, cultivated prose as other writers have cultivated poetry. It has the merit of having served as a text for other analyses of prose-style than mine. Saintsbury says of the passage that it is 'a perfect type in miniature of rhythmic prose'; and to this I add that its qualities of excellence are not exhausted in its rhythm. But here it is:

And her eyes if they were seen would be neither sweet nor subtle; no man could read their story; they would be found filled with perishing dreams and with wrecks of forgotten delirium.

It is impossible, of course, to separate actually the various qualities (or, as they may be called, instruments in the orchestra) that make up a piece of fine prose; but as the ear can isolate, even in an orchestra, one instrument after another, and attend to it while still remaining aware of the whole of which each instrument is a part, so it is possible imaginatively to isolate and to attend to every quality in prose. The first quality to which attention may be drawn is the quality of vowel sound. Vowels play a very large part in the magical effect of sound in general. They are more primitive than consonants, and probably express, or at least reveal, a deeper layer of consciousness. One object, therefore (whether deliberate or instinctive), of every writer is to select such vowel sounds as will induce in his reader the mood appropriate to the nature of his subject and favourable to its reception. In verse it is done in the main by assonances and by regular patterns of vowel sounds; but in prose, the rule is that there should be no apparent rule; in short, that there should be, above all, variety in harmony. Setting out now the vowel sequence in the above passage, we see it as follows:

á é ĭ í ā é éé ē ōō ē ĭé ē ó úé;   ō á ōō ē āī óí;   ā ōō é ou í í éíí ē á í é ó óóé éííú

Observe, first of all, the variety of vowel sounds here present. Few, in fact, are missing. Next note that though not regularly recurring, each, with one exception, occurs more than once. Finally it will be observed that the tendency is from long to short, from suspense of sound to activity. It is as if in the first part of the sentence the mind were being deliberately kept up; and, in the second, as if it were being rolled rapidly down.

The next quality is that of the consonant-sounds; and the scheme of the passage is as follows:

nd hr z f th wr sn wd b nthr swt nr stl; n mn cd rd thr str; th wd b fnd fld wth prshng drms nd wth rks v frgtn dlrm.

Here, again, is a most interesting combination of sounds, the outstanding characteristic of which is, again, variety in harmony. As in the vowel sequence there is, at the ·same time, a progression. The tendency in the earlier parts of the passage is in the direction of softness; it is as if the mind were walking on the tip of the lips, fearful of what it is about to discover; the consonants are light and soft-spoken. Towards the end, however, not only do the words themselves become longer, but the consonants grow deeper and heavier, culminating in the gutturals of 'wrecks' and 'forgotten'.

Now look at the passage as a piece of rhythm—with all sound and sense for the moment submerged in the movement. It can be indicated in this way:

la la lá | la la la lá | la lá | la la lá | la lá | la lá la | lá lá | la lá |
la lá la | la la la lá | la | la lá la la | lá | la la lá | la la lá la | la lá la-la ||

Hours might profitably be spent upon the rhythm here revealed; but my purpose is not to exhaust the subject but to open it. Note, then, first, the variety of the rhythms employed: they vary from rhythms of one beat to rhythms of four; and only a few of them occur more than once, but these very significantly. They are the opening and the closing rhythms respectively. The triple foot, la la lá, occurs three times—each time as an opening; and the triple foot, la lá la, likewise occurs three times, and each time as a close. If you will repeat these rhythms you will hear that the first as naturally opens as the second naturally closes the mind. Having such a rhythm as la la lá, you cannot imagine that the subject is done with; and having such a rhythm as la lá la, you cannot imagine there is any more to be said. They are head and tail, and nobody can make them change places without destroying the life of the passage.

Consider, now, the variety of pitch. Having read the passage several times to be able to listen to oneself reading it, you will observe that the voice drops steadily and progressively through the three phrases. The first phrase, beginning with 'And her eyes' and ending with 'subtle', is comparatively high; it is in the mood of expectancy, of wonder, of suspended yet inquiring attention. The second phrase is lower; it adds to the mystery without resolving it; it intensifies the mood of quiet tragedy. The third phrase is lowest of all, and by the time the voice has reached the word 'delirium', the pitch is at the nethermost end of sound. This 'fall' is in complete harmony with the progression already noted of vowels and consonants. They conspire together to produce the single effect of suspense followed by anxiety and resolved in horror. The passage simply cannot be read in any other way, or to produce another effect. Such was the effect intended, and such is the effect that is produced.

Other 'instruments' could be singled out and listened to, but the present analysis may be closed with a note on the 'meaning' of the passage. There is a perfectly logical order of feeling discernible in it: a progress of the heart as well as of the head. In the opening phrase the mind is in a state of inquiring suspense. Regarding the object before it, and guessing, as it were, at its nature, the mind reports first a negative conclusion. Such eyes, it says, would, if I could only examine them, prove to be neither sweet nor subtle. In the second phrase the mind comes to a further conclusion, to the conclusion that the eyes are mysterious beyond its comprehension. Not only are they neither sweet nor subtle, but they are not to be described in intelligible terms. Hence the sympathetic reader is being prepared for the description that afterwards appears in the third phrase. In this phrase the mind resolves its doubt concerning the intelligibility of 'her eyes', and concludes that they can only be described in terms of dreams and delirium. The process has been orderly. The mind first suggests, afterwards to reject, the intelligent hypothesis that the eyes may be either sweet or subtle. Next, it despairs of intelligible comprehension, and declares that they are not to be described or understood by human intelligence. Finally, it does describe them, but in the language of dream and of non-human consciousness. And this logic proceeds step by step with the development of the sounds, both vowel and consonant, as well as with the order of the rhythms. Each instrument, in short, has a single aim, but an aim that is likewise common to them all.

THE BIG BOW-WOWS

The military critic of the *Times* thinks no small beer of himself; and the *Times* thinks no small beer of him; and I am given to understand that even when his style is at its best, the Government trembles at his nods. Being myself a literary critic whose judgement of the military efficiency of Colonel Repington must needs be only of that part of his total efficiency which I profess to understand, I think merely Government ale of him—a beverage, which I have authority for saying, stands to small beer as small beer stands to wine. It is not that the military critic of the *Times* cannot write in the sense of conveying his ideas. Who could not convey the ideas of the military critic of the *Times,* provided he confined himself to a modest style and vocabulary, such as was adopted, let us say, by Wellington and Julius Cæsar? This

style, clear, workmanlike, soldierlike, was perfectly adapted
to military service; and fitted the art of war as closely as the
rest of the military accoutrements. Such military critics
carried their vocabulary in their knapsacks; and every word
and phrase of it was chosen for its military serviceability.
But the military critic of the *Times* is not content to write
in the military tradition. Julius Cæsar must invade the
literary territory and attempt to write as he fancies writers
write. He must aim at embellishing his prose, dressing it up
in civilian finery and setting it to dance. Good Heavens,
how he does it! But a truce to introductions, behold the
style himself. Enter the military correspondent of the *Times*
with a report of his ceremonial visit to the King's Fleet. His
dispatch bears the address 'In Northern Mists'; and it opens
as follows:

When the grey grim forms of the King's Grand Fleet loom up
before us in these Northern latitudes, they convey to us a sense
of power that no one can dispute. Line after line, in ordered
majesty, great ships and small, they stretch away further than the
eye can reach, and as the vastness of the mighty armament becomes clear to us the terrible character of this tremendous
instrument of war leaves beholders dumb.

Well, now that you have read it, what do you think of it?
I know what I think of it; but my readers' opinion may be
different. They may be of opinion that it is fine writing; the
Times is undoubtedly of that opinion; so is Colonel Repington; and so, I imagine, will be the Government and forty-five
and a half million of the population—including all those
who like their prose written in verse. And, surely enough,
if to write fine is to write à la Colonel Repington, the foregoing passage is not, as I think it, all at sea, but monstrous
fine. May we, however, presume to examine it? May we
take it out of its glass case and blow on it a little? May we
inspect its splendour?

The first thing that strikes the ear is the trot of the accustomed verse-forms. Trot, did I say? Here is a whole herd of horses trotting—sea horses, perhaps, or, may I say, the horse and feet of an army?

When the grey grim forms of the King's Grand Fleet.

There's a grand opening for you: diddi dum dum dum, diddi dum dum dum. It is like the prelude to a recitation by Mr. G. R. Sims. But this is followed by a horse of another trot altogether, by a hexameter line which Mr. Bridges will do well not to envy:

Loom up before us in these Northern latitudes.

Exhausted by his efforts to write in several styles of meter at once, our author sinks into prose for the next phrase, but a prose so nearly allied to blank verse that a stricter ear than his own might claim it for verse:

They convey to us a sense of power.

It is almost Wordsworthian; but not, I think, quite. In compensation, the metrical form is immediately recovered; and the sentence closes with the perfect line:

That no one can dispute.

Three lines of verse with the fourth a promising candidate for the bays is not bad for a single prose sentence. Can our author keep it up? The next sentence opens well:

Line upon line, in ordered majesty.

Splendid, and at the same time, suble with *double entendre*. For to what other lines, in what other ordered majesty, than the lines and majesty of ships is not Colonel Repington hinting at? Here, as plainly as good taste may dare, we are called to read between the lines and to enjoy the æsthetic spectacle of a fine writer constructing his line upon line in ordered majesty in onomatopœia with the naval lines he is describing. Is it not excellent? Then comes another line—a different trot again. What, has this author all the King's horses at his command?

> Great ships and small.

Coleridgian, by my halidame. Coleridgian or Mr. Guy Thorne—one or the other, I am sure. Ah, but invention flags in the next phrase. We are in prose again. But not for long. No, no; Pegasus is merely taking his oats for some new leap in the air. Listen to the beatings of his mighty wings:

> The vastness of the mighty armament.

Shakespearian, sir, perfect Shakespearian. Count the feet of this noble trotter. They are precisely ten in number, and not a toe missing. It is a line to repeat in one's dreams: 'The vastness of the mighty armament'. Mortal man cannot be expected, even when writing in Northern mists, to maintain this altitude of inspiration; and, indeed, the fog comes into Colonel Repington's throat and his muse slackens rein. 'Becomes clear to us the terrible character' is pedestrian. Alas, it is prose; it is even banal prose. What a fall, oh, what a fall! But our gallant Colonel is soon up again. From the prose to the sublime is only a kick; and in the very next phrase we are winging the empyrean once more in blank verse:

> Of this tremendous instrument of war.

After this, what does art demand but a solemn close, something suggestive of the grandeur and sadness of the mighty lines we have criticised? And here it comes; spondee (for so I take it); amphibrach; spondee (for so I take it):

> Leaves beholders dumb.

Dum, didumdi, dum.

But to what purpose should attention be drawn to the silly assonance of latitude and dispute; grim and grey; ships and small; stretch and reach; tremendous instrument, etc.? Are they not audible to the horseman's ears? Cannot even Sister Anne hear them coming? Are they not in Colonel Repington's own phrase 'instinct with vitality and go'? Do they not leap to the lug? What I may observe, however, is the utter failure of the author to convey to *us* the sense of power which the Navy, he tells us, conveyed to him. It is a sense of power so moving that 'no one can dispute it'. You have only to see it to be impressed. The eye cannot reach to the end of the line, yet all the same 'the vastness becomes clear to us'. Finally for all our expectation we are left only with this assurance, that the spectacle 'leaves beholders dumb'. And, indeed, what other evidence do we need of it? Colonel Repington is dumdidumb.

WHAT A STYLE CAN DO TO LETTERS

Mr. Gosse's Address on the occasion of the bi-centenary of Sterne contained nothing new, but a great deal that was true. Sterne's style, he said, was the best conversational style in the language; and appearing when it did it assisted in the break-up of the rhetorical manner of composition. For this, however, in my opinion, we have had to pay rather dearly. A stricter sense of taste would merely have added the conversational style to our language without sacrificing to it the rhetorical style which for certain subjects and in certain moods is necessary. The effect of Sterne was to laugh rhetoric down, not entirely to the conversational level, but half-way, and to create thereby the compromise of styles familiar in the leading article of journalism. He would be a bold man who dared, and a great man who could, restore the rhetorical style to English; and at present I see no likelihood of it.

Nevertheless, the style is legitimate and even noble. In a greater age we shall certainly recover its use.

THE EFFECT OF SATIRE

Satire arises from noble hatred and it inspires ignoble fear. It is welcomed when it misses the mark, and it is boycotted when it reaches home. The satirist is never under any circumstances an object of admiration, either to his victims or to their friends or even to their enemies. Everybody, in short, conspires to hate the satirist, save only the few whose feelings are as much moved as his own. The first symptoms of the presence of great satire are the congregation of persons formerly distant and opposed, and their conjoined shouts of each other's merits; for then is the time for all the mediocre to stand together. It is amusing on this account to hear the mediocre now calling for satire to come and rend them: as if the experience would be a happy one for them. But if they tell the bushes that they are looking for wars, we may be sure that they have not yet heard the guns over the hills.

Susceptibility to satire, however, implies some moral feeling, the sense of shame at least; and of this in every age some men are destitute. There was a public man in Juvenal's day who recited Juvenal's verses on himself in public and thought himself untouched because nobody saw any wounds, unaware that the absence of feeling implied death. There are such men to-day, whom scorpions cannot harm, nor whips cause to flinch.

ON ESSAY WRITING

I doubt the power of any manual to teach people who cannot write to write; but predestined writers may learn many of

the tricks of the trade from reading what the professors
have to say of it. Such instruction is overheard rather than
heard, as the best instruction usually is. The 'don'ts' enumer-
ated in this little volume[1] are numerous and, on the whole,
sound—if only they are understood; but the commandments
are lacking in energy. The art of writing, for example, is
defined as 'the conveying of one's own thought to the mind
of another'. But how dull, how pedestrian! Merely to
convey thought is not an art but a craft, if not a trade. There
is as much difference between writing as an art and writing
as a means of utilitarian communication as between painting
a picture and a door. Art includes utility, but it also trans-
cends utility. Over and above the desire to communicate
thought, there is for the artist as writer the desire to make
it prevail in the minds of others; in short, art is a means of
power. I should say that the end of the writer is to be able
to produce by means of written words *any* effect he desires
in the minds of others. To express himself is not enough: he
wishes to impress himself; and words are the instruments
of his magic. That this desire to subject other minds to his
own is really the motive of the writer as artist is proved by
the natural suspicion in which a writer who threatens to
become successful is held by his first readers. Readers feel
towards him the repulsion as well as the attraction of the
snake for the bird. Power they instinctively feel is there, and
they are afraid of it. Style is only the device adopted by great
writers to make their power more attractive than repulsive;
style is power made gracious.

The essay is no longer cultivated; but it grows wild in
great profusion. As easy to write as a sonnet, the essay is at
the same time as difficult a form to perfect. Mere ease of
writing (or of reading either) is no proof of the possession
of a style; and it is a fact that the emptiest and least satisfying
of modern writers are easy and even pleasant to read. None

[1] *A Manual on Essay Writing.*

is more so, perhaps, than 'Alpha of the Plough'; and none
answers better to the description I have just given. We are
told that 'Alpha of the Plough' is a 'well-known author who
prefers to write under a pen-name in order to say what he
chooses'. Expectant of revelations, or at least, of candour
beyond the discretion of a 'well-known author', we read
the essays only to find ourselves asking what need for con-
cealment there was. There is nothing that might not be
signed by any of a hundred 'well-known authors' without
risking his reputation, either for discretion or the commonplace. It is all perfectly respectable and perfectly superficial.

The 'well-known author' knows the rudiments of his
trade, and is well-practised in them. But the very skill of it
becomes monotonous and ceases to give the pleasure art
owes us, when we find one phrase succeeding another with
the regularity and punctuality of a good train service. Take
this rather long extract, for example, and examine it:

But if the solitude of Ypres is memorable, the silence is terrible.
It is the silence of imminent and breathless things, full of strange
secrets, thrilling with a fearful expectation, broken by sudden
and shattering voices that speak and then are still—voices that
seem to come out of the bowels of the earth near at hand and
are answered by voices more distant, the vicious hiss of the
shrapnel, the crisp rattle of the machine-guns, the roar of 'Mother'
that sounds like an invisible express train thundering through the
sky above you. The solitude and the silence assume an oppressive
significance. They are only the garment of the mighty mystery
that envelops you. You feel that these dead walls have ears, eyes,
and most potent voices, that you are not in the midst of a great
loneliness, but that all around the earth is full of most tremendous
secrets. And then you realise that the city, as dead as Nineveh to
the outward eye, is the most vital city in the world. One day it
will rise from its ashes, its streets will resound once more with
jests and laughter, its fires will be relit, and its chimneys will
send forth the cheerful smoke. But its glory throughout all the
ages will be the memory of the days when it stood a mound of

ruins on the plain with its finger pointing in mute appeal to heaven against the infamies of men.

I imagine that when our 'well-known author' brought his essay on 'A City That Was' to the conclusion just quoted, he put down his pen with a feeling of considerable satisfaction. Running his mind and eye over the general form, he could fairly flatter himself that it was complete and smooth and beyond the criticism of any of his fellows. The opening contrast of solitude and silence had been duly recalled some half-way through the passage and brought to a climax in paraphrase in the concluding sentence. Adjectives and nouns had been properly paired off. Onomatopœia, alliteration, cadence, variety of sentences, and all the other tricks of the trade had been neatly attended to. And, finally, the atmosphere had been skilfully sustained by a succession of words in the same key, broken only, and quite properly, by the sudden and shattering discords that represent the bursting of shells and the noise of guns. Yes, it was a good piece of workmanship, and had all the trade finish. But how much delight can we get out of it? The delight of literature being essentially the unexpected pleasure provided for us, we can classify literature according to its yield of this quality. Some literature delights us once, and on a superficial reading, and then is exhausted. Literature of a higher order delights us over and over again before finally we are done with it. But literature of the very highest order is a perpetual source of delightful surprise that keeps us in a state of constant wonder. In the passage I have quoted, there is not a single delightful surprise from the first phrase to the last. All runs with the smoothness, but also with the expectedness of machinery. It is a lathe turning out phrases and words and thoughts that we are witnessing; it is certainly not an artist quiring like the cherubim. Analyse the sentences one by one; and ask yourself if they contain a turn of phrase or even a word that is not taken from the shop-window. The

E

solitude is memorable, the silence is terrible. There are imminent and breathless things, strange secrets, fearful expectations, oppressive significances, great lonelinesses, tremendous secrets, mute appeals. Not only anybody could have said as much, but anybody would—somebody only would have said it differently. And the impression conveyed is of the same order as the writing that conveys it; we are not in the least surprised to hear that Ypres is like that; we expected it to be like that; and we could very well have described it in the same manner without ever going to see it or hearing from a 'well-known author' who has, he tells us, been there. But all this is to say that the description is not authentic, it is not original, it communicates no fresh feeling; in a word, it is not literature.

A LESSON FROM FRANCE

Beyond their personal interest, the *Love-Letters of Juliette Drouet to Victor Hugo* have an interest which, if not literary, is at least psychological. They number in all some two thousand and cover a period of fifty years of devoted fidelity. One of the first, written in 1833, contains this passage: 'I love you, ergo I am faithful to you, touch only you, desire you, dream of you; in a word, I love you and that means everything'. And the last, written in 1883, the year of her death, is as follows: 'I am proud and happy to sign my life certificate with this one word; I love only you'. Such a constancy of love would seem impossible to a woman, and a Frenchwoman, of Juliette Drouet's early life and character. An illegitimate child, she was the mistress of several men and a favourite of the stage before she met Hugo, and everything in her appeared to point to a fresh conquest quickly forgotten. Yet she not only gave up the stage at his jealous suggestion, but retired into comparative solitude, where for fifty years her only occupations were to wait for Hugo's visits and in the intervals to write these letters. It might have been thought that in France, the courtesan of the nations, such constancy would be ridiculed or its existence made impossible. On the contrary, it is France that has given the world the greatest love-letters ever written—the six letters exchanged between Abélard and Héloïse—and now presents us with the devoted letters of Juliette Drouet. Far from ridiculing romantic love, when it really exists, the French generally pay too much homage to it. The reason is that the French have, after all, only a talent for love; but a talent they take the utmost pains to cultivate. They are thus much gratified when they can point to a work of art in this field, and spare no pains either to produce it or to kill with criticism anything that is below their polished level. The English, on the other hand, having a natural genius for love (shown in our incomparable lyric traditions), think, in the significant phrase of Morris, that 'Love is enough'. Their neglect to cultivate it is almost as much a national habit as the French habit of intensive culture. Assuming too hastily that love comes by nature and needs not to be perfected by art, they are at once the best and the worst lovers in the world. It is in love as it would have been in our literature if the Elizabethan period had passed without criticism. In other words, our criticism of love has not yet begun. The elevation of these letters of Juliette Drouet is not great. Like most of the published English love-letters, they contain too many trivial references for a severe taste. In this respect they are much below the classic of France.

'The love of economics,' said Mr. Shaw in a rare moment of illumination, 'is the mainspring of all the virtues.' Very well, then, we can look for the mainspring of Love in it, can we not? From this point of view I should like to read an essay on the Sociological Value of Love. In a pamphlet called *The Fruit of the Tree*, Mrs. Flora Annie Steel defines

Love as 'that curious fig-leaf of the mind with which
Humanity has sought to hide its sin', and she makes it
evident that her ideal is heaven where is neither male nor
female, neither marrying nor giving in marriage. A noble
ideal too; but I am not so sure that the shortest way to it is
not the very Love which she appears to despise! For Love
has nothing to do with marriage in the ordinary sense, and
perhaps as little to do with sex at all. Nevertheless, its utility
here upon the earth may still be great, though itself have no
earthly value. How is that? you ask. As a direction, I reply.
There is an analogy between Truth and Love which ought
to be pointed out. Nobody yet spoke words of absolute
truth, which, indeed, is unattainable; but the passion for
truth does result in positive approximations. Similarly,
nobody ever yet has known Love, which is, equally with
Truth, unattainable; but the passion for love does result in
positive approximations which themselves are not to be
despised. And, as in a period of intellectual decadence, it is
well that the unattainable ideal of Truth should be preached
—even at the risk of the martyrdom of its apostles—so in a
period of sexual decadence it is well that the unattainable
ideal of Love should be preached—at the risk of no matter
how many killed and wounded among its disciples. I should
say myself, as a humanist, that the characteristic phenomenon
of the last quarter of a century has been the fall in the price
of women's sex. Sex has not had set upon it during these
years, either by men or by women, anything like the social
price it commanded in the early days of Queen Victoria.
Then the price of women's sex was marriage at the very
least; and, in the case of women of good taste, love in
addition. Before the war, on the other hand, it neither
demanded nor commanded either except amongst the few.
But this was not a state of things that ought to have continued,
however it might seem to Mrs. Steel and other immature
mystics the herald of a new step in evolution or what not.

And as War came to remind Men that they were men, Love must come to remind Women that they are women. War as a sociological phenomenon is a costly device for restoring to men their pride and self-respect. Love is a device for restoring to women theirs. And if a man finds delight in giving his life for 'Honour' (another abstraction by the way), women ought to refuse their sex for anything less than 'Love'.

The common assumption that love is a sort of wild-flower, like, say, lady's smock, that best grows without culture and withers the hour it is plucked, is responsible for a good deal of the mawkishness, on the one hand, of English love, and of its hypocrisy on the other. Stendhal noted that the English fear to cultivate love lest they should display vulgarity, and in the attempt to avoid vulgarity they often fall into 'abominable affectation'. Its alternately wild and withered characters amongst us are also responsible for much more than the professed contempt of love in general. It makes for unintelligence in other areas of life as well. After all, we can only think as deeply as we feel; and if we deliberately shallow our feelings for fear of making fools of ourselves, we shall equally shallow our thoughts. The greatest intelligences—men, that is, who have thought and felt most deeply—have always, it may be observed, been as much concerned about Love as about Truth. Plato rises to the mind. There is the marvellous *Journal to Stella*. Vyasa, the author of the *Mahabharata,* has some wonderful chapters on it. Stendhal himself, though not of the highest order, kept himself well balanced by an equal attention to criticism and romance.

English readers prefer love to be treated in one of two ways: the animal or the divine; and in both our literature excels. The French, on the other hand, prefer to live in the midway region where neither real innocence nor real bestiality is possible. They are human, all too human for us.

Stendhal's treatment of love is at once realistic and idealistic; not, as ours, both alternately. He can thus be serious about it longer than most English writers without either boring or disgusting us.

IRELAND: DIAGNOSES

Somewhere in his *Reveries over Childhood and Youth,* Mr. W. B. Yeats remarks on a difference between Englishmen and Irishmen. You may live with an Irishman for years without learning anything of his private affairs, while often an Englishman will take you into his confidence after only a few minutes' acquaintance. The observation may be correct, but Mr. Yeats himself certainly does not support it; for never in any volume of personal recollections have I read anything more strictly intimate and personal than in Mr. Yeats' present *Reveries.* A mere Englishman like myself does not know, when reading some of his pages, where to look for embarrassment. Is it egotism—as his father told him—or naïveté that made him do it? In any case, however, the light his confessions throw upon Mr. Yeats himself is a little too domestic for my appreciation. Such life of thought and emotion as he has had is certainly obscured by incidents which figure, of necessity, larger in this book than in Mr. Yeats' own mind. How to write the story of one's childhood —one's first childhood, I should say of Mr. Yeats—is, indeed, a problem of art. But Mr. Yeats has made it a work of artlessness. And the effect is not to reveal the germination of a poet's temperament, but to portray on an isolated and meaningless canvas a figure, rather pitiable than admirable—a figure, moreover, which reveals nothing beyond itself. Here and there in this medley of recollections and reveries, however, we come upon a chance remark which we can, if we like, turn to intelligent account. Quite naïvely, for instance, Mr. Yeats wonders whether 'the delight in passionate men in his plays' is anything more than a memory of his terrible old grandfather. That puts us, perhaps, upon the scent of a particular quality in Mr. Yeats' work—its pose, as of an attitude imitated and acted under the almost hypnotic constraint of some alien will. When you read Mr. Yeats, are you not aware of a voice that is not his own, but another's speaking and acting through him? Is Mr. Yeats much more than a conscientious medium of his grandfather, his father, and such other people as have impressed him? These questions open out still more widely. Possibly the whole of the modern Irish school is really in a kind of catalepsy, and all its works are only reveries over childhood and youth?

There is a kind of 'playboy' in every Irish writer whose sallies into the ordered mind are as frequent as they are productive of incongruity; and it is with the utmost difficulty and self-restraint that even the most conscientious of Irish writers (Æ for instance) keep their 'playboy' under control. Swift managed to do it perfectly, so that you may read an essay like that upon the 'Conduct of the Allies' and not discover in the whole course of it a single sentiment out of place, either of highfalutin or of whimsicality, or a single jar upon perfect propriety. But Swift only managed it by exercising his 'playboy' in other affairs—in constructing ingenious Latin puzzles, for example, or in inventing elaborate plays upon words. By this means he kept his 'playboy' busy, and was thus at liberty to write his serious essays without Handy Andy's interruptions. Mr. Shaw, who in some respects has a mind like Swift's, has never found an engrossing pastime for his imp of incongruous mischief, who is therefore left free to intrude himself and his comments into conversations where he is absurdly out of place. Occasionally, perhaps, as when a spoiled child joins in the conversation of his elders, the 'playboy' makes a remark the humour of which carries off the incongruity—Mr. James Stephens is more often fortunate in this respect than any other Irish writer—but usually the child is a bore with whom one must laugh to conceal one's embarrassment. To know how to treat his 'playboy' is the first duty of the Irish writer. He must not suppress him altogether, for that is to become an imitation Englishman—Mr. Boyd, by the way, is wrong in regarding Swift as one of England's writers; no man was ever more Irish or wrote better English! On the other hand, he must be careful not to indulge him, lest he should spoil by his intrusions the tone of Irish writing. A delicate enough task, and one that requires a perfect taste to carry through. In the meanwhile, an English critic is not to be despised as a tutor to the child.

AN IRISH NATIONAL LITERATURE

English, for all that it is spoken and written by the inhabitants of England—for the most part badly—is an excellent language, since Sanskrit, the best, perhaps, that has ever been created. There is nothing to prevent the Irish from excelling the English in its use; and in these days, indeed, it is an easy task. But what a re-conquest would be involved in that—to take the language of the English and to better the instruction! Great Irishmen, moreover, are there to prove that a profound Irish national sentiment is not incompatible with a resolution to beat the English at their own tongue. Swift was at least as patriotic an Irishman as any modern Sinn Feiner; his *Drapier's Letters* in defence of Ireland were modelled on Demosthenes, and had all the patriotic passion of the Philippics. Yet he wrote an English which, for simplicity, strength and purity, is the despair of English writers.

Again, English is by no means an exhausted language, or a language incapable of receiving new impressions. It is still in the youth of its art; and I can enumerate several qualities that are still latent in it, and still, therefore, to be drawn out. For instance, easy lucidity is as yet a rare effect in English writing; and it is pre-eminently one that the Irish genius is fitted to produce and to perfect. For the Irish genius is a genius for talk; and cultivated talk is the very substance of easy lucidity in literature. Again, I am perpetually being struck in reading modern Irish writers by an effect of English words which no Englishman to my knowledge has ever succeeded in producing, a caressingly melancholy intimacy as between the reader and the writer. It is rarely that two English friends can converse upon some past tragedy—even that of their own lives—without awkward pauses, or still more awkward phrases. Words do not fail them but their English does. The very intonation of their voices upon such occasions seems to warn them that they are about to make fools of themselves; in other words, that they are reaching the end of their tether in language. The Irish, on the other hand, are masters in such moods. Where the English become dumb or stilted, the Irish begin to find themselves at ease. This quality is, therefore, peculiarly open to Irish writers to develop. It is a province that is altogether theirs for the taking. And what of their gift of fancy? I have said that there is a 'playboy' in every Irishman; and that the use he makes of his 'playboy' is the test of the Irish writer. Mr. Boyd understands me as having referred to the Handy Andy of Lever, and to the stage-Irishman of the nineteenth century. But my reference to Mr. James Stephens, who is no stage-Irishman, might surely have saved me. Mr. James Stephens exemplifies my 'playboy' theory both as to its evidence and in its application. The 'whimsiness' of Mr. Stephens is as far removed from Handy Andyism as from anything English. At the same

time it is still only an imperfect and embryonic manifestation
of the spirit of humour which I regard as peculiarly Irish.
Had Mr. Stephens the genius of the English language to his
tutor, he would, I think, make of his gift of humour a
unique masterpiece in English literature. As certainly as
Rabelais, by virtue of his inspiration, drew out of the French
language a single quality and universalized it—in other words,
made it common property to writers in French—yet in
such a manner that nobody can say whether Rabelais invented or discovered the quality, whether French spoke through
Rabelais or Rabelais through French—so certainly could an
Irish writer like Mr. James Stephens universalize in English
the quality of whimsiness. Is all this creation within the
limits (if there are limits) of English so small a task that
Irish writers should despise it? Are they afraid of losing their
nationality in English? But if their nationality is, as they
claim, real, it is, unless past its prime, still creative; and it
has, therefore, nothing to fear save its fear. And it would
remain Irish in English not a whit the less for surrendering
itself to the Muses that preside over English literature. The
contrast between the attitude of the Irish writers whom
Mr. Boyd defends and the attitude of those Irish writers
whom I am bespeaking is expressed in the contrast of the
spirits of Caliban and Ariel. Caliban is Ariel nursing his
grievance. Ariel is Caliban with his grievance sublimated.

After Mr. Boyd's warning note in *Ireland's Literary
Renaissance,* I risk being taken up for trespass. 'The main
purpose of the Literary Revival', he says, 'has not been to
contribute to English literature, but to create a national
literature in Ireland. . . . The provincial Irishman is he who
prefers to identify himself with the literary movement of
another country than his own.' This, I take it, means that
we who are readers and writers of English have no title to
pass judgement upon the literary work of Ireland; and,

again, that Irish writers who appeal to English readers are by that very fact provincialized. The standard of judgement for Irish writers, even though they write in English, is the standard of Irishmen in Ireland. What the latter like is good Irish literature; and what they do not like is merely English. But this turning of the tables upon English literature is a little more than I am prepared to sit under. My contention is that whatever is written in English may fairly be judged by the standards of English, though it should happen to be written by an Irishman, an Australian, a Canadian, or a Hindu. The facts that the language is English, the grammar English, the syntax English, the vocabulary English, are enough in my opinion to warrant a judge of English in proceeding to pass sentence upon it.

This is not to say that there may not be in a localized English literature a particular flavour characteristic of the local genius. We know that in several of the counties of England there are writings in dialect which, though English, appeal particularly and even exclusively to the Englishmen of those counties. Barnes, for example, will never be fully appreciated (for all his inclusion in the *Golden Treasury*) outside of Dorsetshire; and in Yorkshire and Lancashire there are popular dialect writers whose works are unintelligible in the South. But it is certain that Mr. Boyd would claim more than a dialect-value for the writers of Ireland's Literary Renaissance. While modestly disclaiming comparison with writers in the classical English tradition, he insists that the recent Irish school of writers have created a style of composition, both as to form and substance, which differs essentially from English literature, and is consequently not to be compared with it, but which yet is not to be compared with dialect. For my part I cannot conceive what kind of literature written in English can be other than one of the two kinds named. Either it is English literature pure and simple with a special 'note'—Irish, for example, or Scots, or Welsh—or it is dialect literature—literature in the idiom of a particular locality. And, as a matter of fact, the modern Anglo-Irish school of literature is both. On the one side, it is pure or classical English, which can be read by any English reader without a thought of Ireland (I am referring, of course, to its form alone). And, on the other side, it contains dialect-writing or the idiom of the Irish which cannot be mistaken for anything else. As an example of the first, take this splendid passage from the *History of Ireland*, by Standish O'Grady, the 'Father', so-called, of the modern Irish Renaissance. There is nothing peculiarly Irish in its style:

But all around, in surging, tumultuous motion, come and go the gorgeous, unearthly beings that long ago emanated from bardic minds, a most weird and mocking world. Faces rush out of the darkness, and as swiftly retreat again. Heroes expand into giants and dwindle into goblins, or fling aside the heroic form and gambol as buffoons; gorgeous palaces are blown asunder like smoke-wreaths; kings, with wands of silver and ard-roth of gold, move with all their state from century to century; puissant heroes, whose fame reverberates through battles, are shifted from place to place . . . buried monarchs reappear . . . the explorer visits an enchanted land where he is mocked and deluded. Everything is blown loose from its fastenings. All that should be most stable is whirled round and borne away like foam or dead leaves in a storm.

Here, on the other hand, is an example of dialect taken from Dr. Douglas Hyde's translation from Gaelic of the *Songs of Raftery*:

If you were to see the sky-woman, and she prepared and
  dressed,
Of a fine sunny day in the street, and she walking,
And a light kindled out of shining bosom,
That would sight to man without an eye.

There is the love of hundreds in the forehead of her face,
Her appearance is, as it were, the Star of Monday,
And if she had been in being in the time of the gods,
It is not to Venus that the apple would have been given up.

As never a doubt would arise that the first passage I have
quoted is English, never a doubt would arise that this second
is English in the Irish idiom. Yet Mr. Boyd makes no
distinction between them; but assumes that they are both
equally and essentially Irish in character, not to be included
with pure English and equally not to be classed with English
dialect. The first, however, belongs to English classical
literature, and the second to English dialect literature; and
to one or the other, in varying proportions, all modern
Irish literature really belongs.

Mr. Boyd's confusion arises from the admixture of sentimental with critical considerations. As an Irishman jealous
of his nationality and ambitious for the renaissance of Irish
literature, he is naturally desirous of showing that the Irish
genius cannot be hid under the bushel of an imposed and
alien language, but will break through the classical forms
of English and create out of the broken moulds new forms
for itself. It is an admirable aspiration, and Mr. Boyd is to
be praised for possessing it. But may we not point out that
the new forms, when once they are brought into being, are
forms of English? Mr. Boyd has mistaken Irish substance for
Irish form. Because—and it is indubitable—a school of Irish
writers have drawn their inspiration from Gaelic rather than
from Scandinavian, Greek, and Latin sources, he has concluded that they must needs on that account differ essentially
from the classical English writers. But are there no other
schools deriving from other sources than any of these that
yet make no claim to be anything but English? If a school of
English writers should (O most happy thought!) derive
their inspiration from the *Mahabharata,* would they be

justified in acclaiming themselves Anglo-Indian? Mr. Boyd
has permitted himself the uncritical luxury of discriminating
in favour of the Irish over every other form of local English
dialect. There is no doubt it is a luxury; for I confess myself
to a weakness for the peasant idiom which Mr. Douglas
Hyde first wrote down and Synge perfected by art. But
there are other dialects and local idioms, dear and pleasant-
sounding to people familiar with them, which no less than
Irish deserve to be written down and perfected. But no
more ought the Irish than they to be regarded as other than
an English dialect. If these are satisfied with their status as
local modes of English, why not the Irish mode as well?

The penalty of the claim which Mr. Boyd makes for the
Irish school is that Irish writers are protected from genuine
criticism. Thinking of themselves as essentially different
from purely English writers, they ignore purely English
criticism as misdirected and inapplicable to themselves.
What have they to do with the standards of value which
the English apply to professedly English writing? On the
other hand, as Mr. Boyd himself suggests, they are exempt
from each other's criticism by reason of their common need
of a mutual Irish admiration society. Where all the writers
are personally known to each other, frank mutual criticism
is practically impossible, save behind each other's back!
And the only effect of this immunity from open and competent judgement is encouragement to literary perversion,
ending in sterility; I prophesy that the day is not far off when
the modern Irish school will become either English or extinct.

While I am thinking of English literature Mr. Boyd is
thinking of England. England and English literature, however, are separate and distinct from one another; and it does
not in the least follow, because I love English literature, that
I am blind to the crimes of England. Is it of me that even an

Irishman can say that he is Anglo-maniac? Or that he repeats
in the criticism of Irish literature the Anglo-centric attitude
of the English political administration of Ireland? Well,
perhaps it can be said by an Irishman; but it is not true. It is
a matter of no concern to me whether a writer in English
be Irish or Welsh, or Canadian or American, and, as such,
have political, national, or even racial prejudices and prepossessions. All that matters from a literary point of view is
that, whether by accident, force, or by our own consent,
we share a common language, namely, English, the standards, qualities, and potentialities of which we ought in
common to appreciate, respect, and develop. It is just my
complaint that in setting up an Irish literature within English
literature, the Irish propagandists of nationalism with whom
Mr. Boyd sympathizes are putting their political nationalism
before their devotion to the English tongue. They appear
to believe that it is derogatory to them and Irish nationalists
to wish to write in perfect English—not, mark you, in
English that merely pleases and appeals to Englishmen, but
in any style or form of English that can appeal to anybody
but Irish nationalists. And when I remark that this desire to
write in English for Irish political nationalists only is 'provincial', Mr. Boyd tells me that I am adopting the arrogant
attitude of the Castle.

   Mr. Boyd is no less politically-minded in objecting to
my description of the Irish qualities as forming a 'note' in
English literature. That the Celtic influence has before been
felt in English literature, and that it has added a new quality
to our language, he is willing and even proud to admit.
But that what hitherto has been only a 'note'—even such
an exquisite note—should still in these days be no more
than a note, Mr. Boyd does not like to allow, since it appears
to be a reflection upon Ireland's claim to an individuality
separate from that of England. Is it really, however, a

reflection upon Ireland, or upon the Irish race, that, having come to speak a foreign language—a language spoken by millions of people other than the political English—Irish writers should have succeeded in enriching the tongue by a unique contribution? Is the English language so exclusively the property of the English people that Irish writers who have added a new value to it must needs regret their contribution as being a service to the English people merely? I cannot think that Mr. Boyd will be so indiscriminating as not to see that to write excellent English—better English, let us say, than most Englishmen—is neither disloyalty to Ireland nor devotion to England, but simply good literary art.

One of the penalties an Englishman must pay for England's treatment of Ireland is to lie under the suspicion of an Irishman. My reference to the political bias which, in my opinion, is misguiding the Irish Literary Renaissance, has been taken by Mr. Boyd as an insinuation of the charge of treachery. But surely a critic of literature may discover a political bias without being supposed either to have gone in search of it, or to resent it when found. As it happens, I do not resent it in Mr. Boyd in the very least; on the contrary, I sympathize with him in it. If I were an Irishman, I am sure I should *tend* to look at things in much the same light as Mr. Boyd. Having had my own language virtually suppressed, and being compelled to speak and write in an alien tongue, charged with alien traditions, I should feel the inclination to bite my own tongue, and to curse myself for the very ease with which the conqueror's language came to me. And when works of my countrymen, written in this alien language, were claimed for the literature of my conqueror and employed to adorn the triumph of his conquest, my indignation would begin to rise like milk on the boil; and at any moment I might be over the brim and writing nonsense about Ireland's Literary Renaissance.

But feeling, even of this intense and ebullient quality, does not of necessity carry its own justification with it. The heart should always be in flames, but the duty of the head is to remain ice. And it appears to me, after long reflection, that though I write, of course, as an Englishman, I should come to the conclusion that not only was the wrong irremediable, but that perhaps it might be turned to good account. After all, what distinguishes wisdom from folly but the ingenious use that wisdom makes of circumstances that folly cannot employ and only fruitlessly resents? Given that English, by whatever abominable means, has actually now become the predominant language in Ireland; and that nobody either hopes, or in his heart expects, to see Gaelic generally revived as the normal speech of the country —the conclusion to be drawn is that, for better or worse (at the discretion of Irishmen), the future of Ireland is, if not politically with England, at any rate with English literature. Irish writing, by virtue of its use of the English language, is inseparable from English writing in general. Both nations, whether they like it or not, are bound by the genius of what has become their common tongue. And the more frankly Irish writers accept the fact that, since they do not write in Gaelic they must write in English, and hence form a part of English literature, the better for their literary judgement and literary style.

TWILIGHT IN MR. D. H. LAWRENCE

Behind Henry James's novels is an attitude towards life— we need not mind saying a moral attitude, for he certainly had a desire to improve his readers. Behind the novels of Mr. D. H. Lawrence, perhaps the most considerable of the younger school, there is not an attitude simply, but a philosophy. And in his *Twilight in Italy* the philosophy begins to

F

appear. It is crudely expressed, and in some passages Mr. Lawrence is unintelligible; but there can be no doubt of his sincerity and little less of his competence. Mr. Lawrence, it is clear, is one of the few new writers with whom we shall have to reckon. We shall have to beware lest he found a school. But why, it may be asked, beware? The reply is to be found in the character of the philosophy he is defining for himself, the outlines of which are here laid down. For it amounts to a reaction of intellectualism which is not simply corrective of intellectualism but subversive. This volume of essays enables us to form some idea of the damage done by pseudo-intellectuals in the positive reaction towards sensualism for which they may be said to be responsible. Here, with only an equivocal apology, is a return to paganism of the frankest character; and to paganism not as a naïveté but as a cult. Interesting it all is, too, for Mr. Lawrence is something of a genius. His writing is good, his vocabulary is excellent, his style is powerful, and, in time, when he has soaked himself fully in his philosophy, and has come to be able to cover its present nakedness completely, he will prove to be extremely seductive. And what ideas he throws out by the way! Read his first chapter on the Crucifix in Bavaria. It both gives the key to his essays and revives one of the oldest and most sinister interpretations of the Sign of the Cross. Look, again, at his remarkable appropriation to his own use of Blake's symbology in the mysterious poem addressed to the burning Tiger. You will be convinced, unless you are careful, that Mr. Lawrence has almost proved his case—and his philosophy. It is, however, all an error and a reaction. The ecstasy of the senses— let us call it phallic-worship and done with it—is not, as he thinks, of equal worth with the spiritual ecstasy. It is, perhaps, of more than equal worth with the pseudo-ecstasies of the pseudo-intellectuals and pseudo-mystics, who, indeed, well merit to be plunged back into Sheol; but as an

alternative to the real ecstasy that awaits the sincere intellectual and mystic it is a lamentable reaction. We cannot afford
to economize consciousness when reading Mr. Lawrence.

NIETZSCHE: STILL MISUNDERSTOOD

At a recent performance of the *Winter's Tale* in Germany,
a specially written prologue, spoken by Autolycus, referred
to Germany and Shakespeare in these terms: 'This Germany
that loves him most of all, to whom before all others he
gives thanks'. The view that Germany 'discovered' Shakespeare is so common that poor Coleridge is quite forgotten.
Yet it was two years before Schlegel delivered his lectures
on Shakespeare that Coleridge, not more than a stone's
throw from where I am writing, delivered his, in which he
claimed for Shakespeare a judgement equal to his imagination and the rank of 'the greatest man that ever put on and
put off mortality'. True, Coleridge said at the same time
that England, who had been given by Providence the greatest
of poets, had inflicted upon him the most incompetent
critics. But he naturally and justly excepted himself; for
Coleridge was, and knew himself to be, such a critic as
even Shakespeare would have needed no introduction to in
Swift's afterworld. Coleridge's lectures were first delivered
in 1806—they were repeated very often. Over and over
again we have to admire Coleridge's marvellous insight.
Look, for example, at what he says of *Hamlet,* that Hamlet
whom the Freudian school would have us believe entertained
incestuous desires unawares. Coleridge sees in Hamlet's
'aboulia' not an inhibition wrought by some suppressed
desire, but the paralysis of an impulse brought about by a
spiritual shock. There is no other example in Shakespeare's
plays of the incest-motive; it appeared in *Hamlet* once and
once for all. But Coleridge's theory links the Hamlet motive

with two other of Shakespeare's greatest plays—*Othello* and *Lear*. In all three, he says, the tragedy arises from a shock inflicted on a noble nature by an appalling and astonishing treachery, real or apparent; in the case of Hamlet by the treachery of his mother, in the case of Othello by the apparent treachery of his wife, in the case of Lear by the apparent treachery of his daughter. How much more intelligible this is than the theory of Freud-Jones. It covers the facts, it comes within our own cognizance (and Shakespeare is always on the high road of man), and it has, to boot, the countenance of three related plays. Henceforth we need not *argue* with the Freudians, but only *tell* them! In the name of Coleridge, avaunt thee, incestuosity!

Not only did Coleridge precede Germany in the discovery of Shakespeare, but, as I am a critic, he anticipated the thrice-great Nietzsche's doctrine of Dionysos-Apollo. This I supposed was really Nietzsche's discovery; and Miss Jane Harrison, who ought to have known better, in her *Prolegomena to the Study of Greek Religion,* wilfully confirmed my illusion. She, who owed it to us that at least all English references to the Dionysos myth should have been examined by her, overlooked (the careless woman!) the most illuminating reference of Coleridge in these very lectures. 'Dionysos,' he says, 'that power which acts without our consciousness in the vital energies of nature—the *vinum mundi*—as Apollo was that of the conscious agency of our intellectual being'. What could be clearer, or more pregnant of Nietzsche? The doctrine, definition and all, is there in a few words. Did Nietzsche ever read it? Did the Germans, in short, discover Coleridge? We shall never know. But look again at this passage and tell me it is not Nietzsche: 'The Greeks idolized the finite and therefore were the masters of all grace, elegance, proportion, fancy, dignity, majesty. . . . The moderns revere the infinite—hence their passions, their

obscure hopes and fears, their wanderings through the
unknown, their grander moral feelings, their more august
conception of man as man, their future rather than their
past—in a word their sublimity.' Nietzsche might have
written it, might he not? But it was written by Coleridge.
There are many more such pearls cast away in Coleridge;
Nietzsches yet to be will doubtless discover them.

However, I would not put the rediscovery of any truth
ever humanly entertained beyond the reach of Nietzsche.
My respect for him increases with my knowledge of himself
no less than of his Works. It will be difficult, I venture to
say, for any reader of Nietzsche's *Life*, by Daniel Halévy, to
close the last chapter without tears. The spectacle is of a
glorious being dashing his brains out against the bars of
mortality and singing in his agony. The image, if you please,
is monstrous, but so is the spectacle. It is pathos raised to
tragedy. I am most grateful to M. Halévy for saying so little
and yet suggesting so much. In his description of the closing
scenes of Nietzsche's life he has modelled his courtesy upon
that of a certain Lord Coventry who exclaimed to some
courtiers who were pressing for a sight of a noble lord in
tears: 'For God's sake, gentlemen, don't look at a great man
in distress'. Or, perhaps, upon the sublime description of
the death of Socrates by Plato. Or, though less likely, upon
the divine description of the death of Bhishma on his bed
of arrows in Vyasa's *Mahabharata*.

SCHOPENHAUER:
THE MAN BEHIND THE PHILOSOPHY

Read Schopenhauer where you will, it is always a man you
will find. Schopenhauer was more English than German,
and was sure to be among the anti-Prussians. Not only was

he among them, but in Mr. Belfort Bax's essay Schopenhauer's native admiration of England and the English is
clearly brought out. His father designed him to be born in
England and named him Arthur as a consolation for his
wife's failure; he was partly educated in England, and afterwards chose Frankfort to live in because there were so many
Englishmen there. It is not surprising, after this, to discover
that he was as much a personality as a philosopher. Always,
in reading him, you are in conscious contact with a man of
the world as well as with a thinker. Eighteenth-century
England would just have suited him. 'What interested him',
he said, 'were those things alone that concerned men at all
times and in all places'—a definition of the classic. How, you
may ask, is this to be squared with his study of the *Upanishads*
—a literature, dear ninety-nine out of a hundred readers,
that *you* ignore; but of which Schopenhauer said that it was
'the noblest reading in the world and his highest consolation'.
Only that the *Mahabharata* and the *Upanishads* are world-
classics that the world has simply not yet discovered. Plato
had to lie comparatively unknown for nearly two thousand
years—the Indian classics will comfortably lie ten thousand
and still emerge as up to date as ever. Schopenhauer, the
odd explorer, discovered them and became a notable
philosopher on a partial understanding of them. Philosophers
yet unborn will make their reputation out of them.

BOLINGBROKE

As one of the grand dark horses of English history, Bolingbroke will always have an interest for the connoisseurs of
character; but whether he will ever be understood is another
matter. A man of genius who inspired the admiration of
Swift, and almost the worship of Pope; of whom Disraeli
said that he was one of the ablest men that ever lived; a

Voltairean before Voltaire; a modern in the eighteenth century—Bolingbroke baffles definition more by what he failed to do than by what he did. With such gifts as he possessed, with such friends, with such opportunities, it might be thought that there was nothing Bolingbroke might not have done had his heart been set upon it. As it was, any trumpery cabal seems to have been able to embarrass him seriously, and, in the end, to ruin him. I am indisposed, of such a century, to affirm that Bolingbroke's weakness was a too radical scepticism unbalanced (as it was not in the case of Voltaire) by a naturally benevolent heart. Yet there is Burke's satire, on the one hand, and Bolingbroke's life, on the other, to show that his principles were fundamentally anarchic and his conduct without a compass. He appears politically and in every other respect to have been a Machiavellian in a society of simple knaves and fools —but a Machiavellian without a prince's purpose. All his ability, all his genius, all his array of talents, while they could not help but exhibit themselves, failed to produce their maximum effect for the want of orientation. Never at any time (or at any rate for long) did Bolingbroke either wish to do anything or find himself set to do anything. He was essentially one of the great unemployed. As for his style, a little of it goes a long way. It is eloquent, it is witty, it is occasionally grand. But the subject is never quite worthy of it as a whole. A grand style is out of place in a rationalistic exposition; for, on purely rational grounds, passion is an excess, a superfluity. To have Voltairism written in the style of Burke is to have something very near to parody.

LANDOR: THE LOSS OF REALITY

In a good Introduction to an admirable selection from the *Imaginary Dialogues* of Landor, Mr. E. de Selincourt affirms that 'as a writer of prose, none surpassed Landor . . . who gave currency to the ripest wisdom and the noblest reflections'. Wordsworth, Southey, Carlyle, Dickens, Browning and Swinburne were all, he reminds us, impressed by Landor; and he might have added many more. Swinburne compared him with Simonides, Austin Dobson called his prose Greek honey, Carlyle said he was an unsubduable old Roman. W. C. Bennett referred to him as 'the old man eloquent' (Isocrates), Stuart Blackie said he was the most finished master of style that ever used the English tongue, and Mr. Birrell said he 'took pains to be splendid'. After this procession of whirlwind and fire, my still small voice will scarcely be heard; yet I must utter my judgement, which is that all these writers have exaggerated the greatness of Landor.

He has many virtues, his sentences, his choice of words, his elevation of sentiment, are beyond reproach; but there is nevertheless no *virtue* in him. And the reason is that he had no prophetic fire. One single confession reveals this as no analysis could: he hated Plato and regarded him as 'a conceited and self-seeking sophist'. But let me set against him Coleridge's words: 'It might very well be thought serious trifling to tell my readers that the greatest men had ever a high esteem for Plato; whose writings are the touchstone of a hasty and shallow mind'. Landor had not, perhaps, a hasty mind, but shallow it was. Whence, then, came the tributes so freely showered upon him? In an age just about to tumble into the popular period he held himself aloof, and retired, as we know, to an ivory tower in Italy to write to please himself. By contrast with the sweating public educators of his day who were wrestling with wild ignorance in the market place, Landor seemed to them to be an austere god living upon ambrosia in the Isles of the Blest. But it was all an illusion. As far off as he appeared from the world of men he was from the world of reality. No one has ever been warmed or inspired, fed or clothed by him. Far from having given currency to any ripe wisdom, there is no phrase from his prose nor any thought associated with his name that lives. He wrote a few immortal poems— two and a stanza—and these will keep his prose in print. But alive it never will be, for it never was.

WHITMAN IN SHORT

It is possible to regard Whitman from one of two points of view: man and writer. As a man his writings are of interest for their self-revelation, they are documents only. As a writer his personal life is of the smallest concern, but he is of importance as the anti-Euphues of English style. He is the polar opposite of Euphues, as dangerous to be read as Euphues, as mannered, and as much off the highway of English letters. Nobody has ever drunk deep of him without a loss of style. On the other hand, a draught of Whitman now and then is a tonic. This is of his 'poetry' only; his prose, on the other hand, was excellent, some of the best America has produced. What a pity he was not content to write in prose all his life.

SWINBURNE: CHANGELING

Superficial critics of style often lay up for themselves a lot of trouble. Instinctively they assume the right doctrine, namely, that style is the man; and then mistakenly expect their hero to live up to their opinion of his character formed on an imperfect realization of his style. When they learn that in fact their hero was anything but what they supposed, they lay the blame of inconsistency upon him, thus attributing to him the fault of their own laziness or defect of

critical insight. Such a surprise awaited those blind devotees
of Swinburne who chanced to read the article upon him in
the *Spectator*. Sometime during 1862, when Swinburne was
twenty-six and had been two years down from Oxford, he
contributed anonymously to the *Spectator* three articles on
the *Les Misérables* of Victor Hugo. They were absurdly eulo-
gistic of Hugo's style—a thing that can scarcely be said to
exist—but they were much more absurdly critical of Hugo's
humanitarian principles, which were the noblest part about
him. For instance, Hugo defended his work as necessary 'so
long as there shall exist through laws and manners a social
damnation creating artificial hells in the midst of civilization
and complicating destiny, which is divine, with a human
fatality'. Hugo, in short, anticipated Nietzsche in denouncing
the very idea of punishment. But the young Swinburne,
who was shortly to publish *Poems and Ballads,* had neither
then or at any time an ear for so exalted a doctrine. On the
contrary, he defended punishment and deprecated compassion exactly as if he were a magistrate of the bourgeoisie.
The era of Draconian legislation, he urged, which might
conceivably have justified Hugo's outburst, had passed
away; and now that we had an 'efficient poor law', no
possible excuse remained for crime. 'For the man (he said)
who, having the workhouse at hand, prefers stealing to
breaking stones and a contemporary separation from his
family, we confess we have little sympathy'; and he went
on to marvel that Hugo dared to weaken the appeal of 'a
resolute conception of morality' by compassionating any
breach whatever of it. If the excuse of fatality, he concluded,
can be allowed to criminals, then *Christus nos liberavit* has
indeed lost its meaning. Away with such compassion and
let the law take its course! Now is that, I ask, the opinion
that Swinburnians would expect of their idol? And I answer
that it is not; but, on the contrary, that they will be surprised
by it and enough ashamed of it to seek to palliate or explain

it. Yet in my view it is neither surprising nor inconsistent
with Swinburne's whole character. I could, in fact, have
deduced it from his style—that licentious, tyrannical, bully-
ing style! It is only for the superficial to be shocked by such
discoveries.

Æ's notice of Mr. Gosse's *Life of Swinburne* is characteristic
of Æ, true to Swinburne himself, and unique in contemporary journalism. Mr. Gosse's *Life of Swinburne* is one of
the most carefully superficial biographies I have ever read.
It is full of facts, but it contains scarcely a word of truth.
If Mr. Gosse had been commissioned by the most jealous
surviving relatives of Swinburne to write the Life of their
kinsman without giving anybody of the name of Swinburne
the least offence, he could not have performed his task more
discreetly. But as for the Life of Swinburne, a study of
Swinburne, a representation of Swinburne, a portrait of
Swinburne as he was, it is not only unilluminating, it is
misleading. Nothing that we can divine of Swinburne from
his Works was apparently a part of his real life at all; and as
little of his real life as possible is revealed. Better, I should
say, one reading of Swinburne as a revelation of the man,
than twenty Lives of him by Mr. Gosse. Better had such
a Life not been written.

In Æ's short notice are one or two comments upon
Swinburne which are really satisfying, however they may
strike the ordinary reader as extraordinary. Æ says of
Swinburne, that 'if he had been born in Ireland our infallible
psychological instinct would have discovered him to be a
changeling, as Mr. W. B. Yeats undoubtedly is'. And by
'changeling' Æ does not mean something merely fanciful
or metaphorical, but something real, though fairy and
non-human. But are we prepared to listen patiently to such
a view? Yet the remark is made by a man capable of brilliant

common sense; there must, therefore, be something to be said for it, and since the changeling theory is the best I know for the case of both Swinburne and Mr. W. B. Yeats, I content myself with remarking that not all is human that wears a human form. Strange beings are amongst us disguised as men; strange moods that are anything but human have their way with some of us. To be human is to be in a continual state of self-criticism and of self-defence; for the task of being and remaining human is difficult and perilous. But what are the signs, it may be asked, that Swinburne was a changeling? Putting aside his life, the story of which, if it were truthfully told, would be as incredible as a giraffe, there is his work, of which not a line that I can discover has the indubitably human note. What Æ says of this is that Swinburne revelled in technique, that is to say, in rhythm. It was peculiar to him to be guided by sound entirely, the sense being left to take care of itself. I do not say, of course, that in Swinburne's case the sense was nonsense. What I am saying is that he wrote poetry by ear, as certain gifted persons play music by ear. But this sense of hearing, this exclusive attention to and cognizance of the value of sound—a sense in Swinburne so acute that what sounded to him well turned out as a rule to be sound in substance—constituted him the non-human creature Æ declares him to have been. For it is of the nature of an 'elemental' or fairy changeling to differ from humans in its approach or method of arriving at what we call sense. With the great human artists the technique is never obvious; but in the non-human, as well as in lesser artists, the technique or external signs of art are everything. Nobody can read Swinburne without being aware that he is reading rhythm through which, if at all, the sense steals as it were unbidden. But in reading the great poets it is the rhythm that steals upon our ear while the sense is entering our hearts.

There are two ways by which inspiration may enter the brain, which is the instrument of the/mind of man. One way is through the appropriate gate, the other is by what I may call a gap in the hedge. The former is the way found and taken by the great artists in whom the gift of inspiration is something more than a mere gift—it is a faculty, a power within their control, as much their own to employ as the normal powers of the mind. Plato, Milton, and Shakespeare belonged to the order of men whose genius communicated with them through the proper gateways. The second method, however, is something akin to a disease of the brain, or, at any rate, it involves an abnormality of the brain. And, in the case of Swinburne, the disease was manifest. 'The peculiar poetic spirit in him,' says Æ, 'was, I fancy, in some way connected with the psychic disease as the pearl is the product of the disease of the oyster.' And the proof of it is this: that when he was cured (as he was by Mr. Watts Dunton) of his psychic disease (when, as I should say, that gap through which his genius passed into his brain was healed) his poetic gift left him. During the thirty years he lived with Mr. Watts Dunton under his nursing care, Swinburne did not write a poem by the Swinburne of his former self.

MEREDITH: A MISFIT NOVELIST

Of Meredith's novels we must say: No, they will not do, they will not do. Meredith was a misfit as a novelist, too great in some respects, too small in others. Now and again he visibly bursts all the boundaries of legitimate story-telling and rolls in the pastures of the essay, criticism, comedy, and farce. At other times he shrinks to the size of a novelettist or a leader-writer of the *Daily Mail*. When he is in the first mood the influence upon him is unmistakably Carlyle;

when in the second it is the newspaper. Listen first to this, and swear, if you can, that it is not Carlyle at second hand:

Remains of our good yeomanry blood will be found in Kent, developing stiff, solid, unobtrusive men, and very personable women. The distinction survives there between Kentish women and women of Kent, as a true south-eastern dame will let you know, if it is her fortune to belong to that favoured portion of the county where the great battle was fought, in which the gentler sex performed manful work, but on what luckless heads we hear not; and when garrulous tradition is discreet, the severe historic Muse declines to hazard a guess. Saxon, one would presume, since it is thought something to have broken them.

Then read the opening of the second chapter of *Vittoria* and deny if you can that a good ten thousand journalists would have written in the same strain. It is Mr. Hamilton Fyfe to a nicety. But this is not all that should be said of Meredith, for he is something more than a Brummagem Carlyle and, of course, infinitely more than a Hamilton Fyfe. To discover him at his best, however, not his novels need to be scrupulously weighed, but his extravaganza, *The Shaving of Shagpat*. *Shagpat* is one of the English master-pieces of the nineteenth century; and to have written one classic in his half of that century is to have performed a prodigy.

Nobody was more terribly misleading and mistaken on the subject of women than Meredith; he has been a cause of great disaster among both sexes. But *The Shaving of Shagpat*, being not a novel but a deliberate grotesque, is worth re-reading many a time. It was Meredith's first book, and naturally indicated the bent of his genius, which was as decidedly non-human as his admirers believe it to have been human. When I say that Meredith had the genius for the grotesque, I mean by it something utterly different from the decadent. The decadent is the *distortion* of great human ideas;

the grotesque is the *creation* of non-human ideas. Consult for more light upon the subject an article by Mr. W. M. Letts in the *Contemporary Review*. Mr. Letts makes the prevalent mistake of attributing creative artistry to children—it is his mistaken homage to the cult of infantilism—but he makes no mistake in discriminating the sane from the insane in matters of the grotesque and the decadent—altogether a useful article. As I was saying, Meredith was at his best in the world of *The Shaving of Shagpat*. There his Welsh blood —some of the oldest in Europe, and therefore charged with pre-European tendencies—found its proper medium of expression—the extravagant, the non-human, the bizarre, the grotesque. (Note that Mr. Wyndham Lewis is partly Welsh.) But to cast the oblique ray of his vision upon modern European society was not only to see modern society all awry, but to assist in putting it awry.

There is something, shall I call it Welsh, something Owen Glendowerish, in Meredith's style that produces the same effect upon me that the spriteliness of Glendower produced upon Henry. It is not only not English, but it is antipathetic to the English character. Friend Walpole remarked that 'one cannot buffoon like Lucian when one wants to speak daggers like Tacitus'; yet Meredith was always tempted to it and was perpetually falling. I open, for example, the first chapter of *Beauchamp's Career* and come upon a description of much the same state of public excitement we have recently witnessed. Here is a fair sample of it: 'It was the deliberate saddling of our ancient nightmare of invasion, putting the postillion on her, and trotting her along the highroad with a winding horn to rouse old Panic'. What a long-drawn-out pastiche, and how utterly inappropriate to the subject—a catastrophe in Wardour Street! But nobody can deny that it is pure Meredith. Occasionally Meredith writes less like a babu and more like an Englishman. Killick's words to

Dr. Shrapnel conveying the news of the drowning of Beauchamp, for example, are almost perfect. 'Hard' would be better than 'sharp'—but there you are, the choice was again Meredith.

GISSING'S MALADY

Gissing hated the 'people' not for their ignorance, but mainly for the absence of qualities that *money could purchase*. Is not this Philistinism pure and simple? Over and over again he interpolates into a passage of excellent squalor a remark to the effect that money alone would end it all. 'Put money in thy purse,' he makes Athel say in *A Life's Morning*, 'and again, put money in thy purse; for as the world is ordered, to lack current coin is to lack the privileges of humanity, and indigence is the death of the soul'. Gissing had such a belief in the deviltry of poverty that he persuaded himself that a world of villas without poverty would satisfy his soul. But is not that, once more, Philistinism pure and simple? It must be said, however, that Gissing misunderstood himself; for he was not, in fact, the Philistine his exile and immersion in scenes of poverty made him appear. As a sensitive mind ostracized from polite society and condemned to live amongst the poor, he naturally most resented the circumstance that most wounded himself; but his own spiritual self-preservation amid these conditions was a proof that not poverty alone was the cause of the prevailing degradation. It is true he denounced poverty in material things as if it were the sole cause of poverty in spiritual things; but there are many passages to indicate that his satisfaction with humanity would have been little greater if all men were equally well-to-do. This redeems him from the charge of Philistinism in the soul; but a Philistine in the mind there is no doubt he was.

By the Ionian Sea is Gissing at his ripest—for *The Private Papers* were, I think, a little over-ripe. The very autumn of his melancholy was upon them. His account of his ramble in Southern Italy, on the contrary, should have represented, and partly did represent, Gissing's Indian summer. He was where he had all his life wished to be. He was alone. He was comparatively free from money and other troubles. And he delighted in writing. As little melancholy as Gissing was capable of might have been expected of his Ionian diary. And yet we find it saturated with melancholy; and so powerfully as to challenge the reader to a fight to maintain his spirits after only one or two of the eighteen chapters.

Why is this? The incidents of Gissing's travel are not at all unpleasant; many of them are amusing. He met with no depressing misfortunes, and he appears to have enjoyed himself. Despite it all, however, and despite, as well, Gissing's manifest intention to write as cheerfully as he travelled, a heavy air hangs over every chapter, every page and almost every sentence. The secret is to be found in Gissing's prose-rhythm. On analysis, his characteristic 'length' or 'stride' is found to be of an essentially melancholy nature. Try these sentences, for example, taken almost at hazard from widely separated pages, and consider how uniform their measure is; each of them is Gissing in little:

So silent it is, so mournfully desolate, so haunted with memories of vanished glory.

A fisherman's boat crept duskily along the rocks, a splash of oars soft-sounding in the stillness.

But here, as there, one is possessed of the pathos of immemorial desolation.

Quite apart from the reflective content of each of these examples, the sequence of prose-feet in them naturally

G

produces the effect of melancholy. Though Gissing has wished to express the utmost lightness, the rhythm here employed (and habitually employed) by him would have defeated his purpose. It would be as easy to represent Chaminade on a bassoon as gaiety or wit in these measures.

A more detailed analysis would show that Gissing was a writer of a single string. The last form of which he was capable was drama, in which (when it is written at all) each character must speak in its own rhythm. Gissing could no more than Byron manage this, since his own personal rhythm was too inelastic—his imagination too limited and egoistic—to admit new movements. As he was born, so he always remained; he grew up, but he never grew out. Was this the effect, partially at any rate, of circumstances? Both Byron and Gissing were driven inwards by their inappreciative days. Both, consequently, were bent towards the exclusive maintenance of their idiosyncrasies. Appreciation, after all, is a necessity to the personal development of the artist; and, most of all, probably, to the dramatist. Without a general atmosphere of appreciation, genius tends to become either idiosyncratic or simply wilful. The more powerful mind, when surrounded by Philistines, retires within itself and creates works of amazing egotism; the less powerful experiments in all manner of tricks and grotesques as a means to procuring the sunlight of appreciation. Gissing's was one of the more powerful minds. Certainly, as his style shows, he was always repeating himself—like an imprisoned soul treading always the selfsame wheel. The monotony is depressing, and adds its powerful melancholy effect to the choice of rhythm. As a last example, look upon this opening passage of *By the Ionian Sea*. It is the key of which there is practically no variation throughout the whole book. No wonder the mind can take pleasure in no more than a chapter or two of it at a time. There is no movement in it. (I have marked the prose feet as they naturally fall, and would refer my readers to Saintsbury's *Prose Rhythm*.)

This || is the third day || of Sirocco, || heavy-clouded, || sunless. || All the colour || has gone || out of Naples; || the streets || are dusty || and stifling. || I long || for the mountains || and the sea. ||

A study of this passage will reveal more of Gissing than all the biographies written of him. The style is the man.

I possess an old notebook in which I used to copy down, ah, how many years ago, extracts from the books I was then reading. Many pages are filled with passages from the novels of George Gissing, and one of them lies open before me now. 'What I really aim at [it is Harold Biffen speaking in Gissing's best novel, *New Grub Street*] is an absolute realism in the sphere of the ignobly decent. I am going to reproduce it verbatim without one single impertinent suggestion of any point of view save that of honest reporting. The result will be something unutterably tedious; precisely, that is the stamp of the ignobly decent life. If it were anything but tedious, it would be untrue.' This was Zola's doctrine carried out with English thoroughness, and nobody has succeeded better in it than Gissing. All the same, even he failed, for neither are his novels tedious nor are they transcripts of life. Something, as, I believe, Mr. Wells said, and Mr. W. W. Jacobs has proved, was wanting in Gissing's realism: it was an eye for life. It will seem strange to hear Gissing charged with a lack of sympathy with the ignobly decent; yet that is what I could establish against him. If you like, he sympathized too much to understand them; or, still better, he reserved his sympathy for their woes only.

This defect was due, I am sure, to his own colossal self-pity. Asked what Aunt Emily said when she heard of her niece's trouble, the latter naïvely replied: 'Oh, she began to sympathize with herself'. It is a common habit, and Gissing was a victim of it. He could not hear some wretched story without being reminded of his own; and in the flood that then gushed out, himself and the other object were mingled and submerged. That this is not the artist's temperament anybody can see for himself; for the artist must have only so much sympathy as just does not carry him off his feet. To have none, is, of course, fatal; but equally it is fatal to have too much. Here again common sense is the beginning of wisdom, which itself is the foundation of beauty. In *The Private Papers of Henry Ryecroft* the real Gissing appears; and even more clearly to me in his style than in his actual confessions. The latter, it is true, are significant enough; for in one place he affirms that he is 'no friend of the people'. I should think not! For were they not always reminding him of himself? The style, however, is the man; and as a pretty exercise my readers should compare the *Private Papers* with Senancour's *Obermann*. Matthew Arnold speaks rightly of the inwardness, the *austere simplicity*, of Obermann—but who can discern any austerity in the simplicity of Ryecroft Gissing? On the contrary, Gissing's sentiment is always brimming over the rims of his forms. He cannot have done with a statement, but must add paraphrases and parallels to wallow in. 'You tell me [he begins] that money cannot buy the things most precious. Your commonplace proves that you have never known the lack of it. When I think of all the sorrow and the barrenness that has been wrought in my life by want of a few more pounds per annum than I was able to·earn, I stand aghast at money's significance.' So far so tolerably good. But at this point Gissing's bitter memories push open the gates of his art and drown us in mere examples. Turn now to letter *XXIX of Obermann*.

The subject is not dissimilar, but the treatment! And it is
not that Senancour was one of your gay, cynical Frenchmen
—the same that are seldom to be found! Senancour also had
retired a little disgusted with life; Stevenson, who wanted
everybody to warm him, even found Senancour 'cheerless'
and bore Arnold a grudge for recommending him. Yet in
discussing poverty Senancour was as austere as simple, as
sympathetic as restrained. I will add that the *Private Papers*
produced on me much the same effect as Jefferies' *Story of
My Heart*. Neither is written by a man's man; both are
suffering from more than melancholy—a softening of the
sentiments.

JAMES'S PLAY OF MINDS

My wish to say something of Henry James that no critic
has said before has been almost anticipated by Henry James
himself. 'A story that can be told is not worth telling', he
has said. Ah, but thereby hangs a very long tale. What are
Henry James's 'stories' then, if they are not told? I should
say that they are the psychological accompaniments played
by a subtle mind to tunes too familiar to need to be sung.
You have to 'imagine' the implied story while at the same
time you follow Mr. James's concurrent translation of it
into the terms of the next and imaginative form of reality.
But what is the next order of reality? It is, as you choose to
regard it, the projection of the actual—a kind of luminous
mental shadow of the real; or it is the world of which *our*
actual is the shadow and the projection. About which is
which, Henry James, of course, has no doubt. He scarcely
distinguishes between spooks, ghosts, feelings, ideas, and
actual people. The latter are for him a mere focus of the
others, interesting only as pointing to the former. But I said
it was a long tale.

To speak out about Henry James is precisely what his art does not allow us. Even Swinburne could have written nothing about him. 'He gave way,' Henry James makes one of his characters say—and it might certainly be said of himself—'he gave way to notions recommended by their not committing him to a positive approach.' Well, there you have it. The method of Henry James is never to make a positive approach to the subject with which he is dealing: it is always by the circuitous route of his own impression that he leads you to the contemplation of his object. The effect of this is almost to transform actuality, or, rather, to concentrate attention upon its intellectual counterpart, to the comparative neglect of actuality itself. Consider his characters, for example, their doings and sayings. They are realistic, in the sense that such people really exist and do and say the things he makes them do and say; but how thin the material part of them appears—their minds are almost visible through their frames. Henry James was essentially interested in the borderland between the physical and the psychic worlds. With one foot planted firmly in the former, he was always taking a step with the other into the latter. Ghosts, for this reason, interested him; and so, too, did all those characters—artists, children, certain kinds of women— whose lives are passed rather in imagination than in common reality. And how excellently adapted was his style to his subject! On the one hand, nobody could be more colloquial without being vulgar than Henry James. He delighted in using words of the most simple and homely speech. But, on the other hand, the giddy analyses of reflection he built upon them, like castles in the air with their base upon the earth, are as far as thought can climb from the ordinary. Like Jack, he plants his bean in the garden right enough— usually well down in the mud—and then there proceeds from it such a beanstalk as tempts one to climb into a world where everything is at once new and old. But you must cease to observe, when you get there, anything that is external, objective, or material. What you behold is the play of minds in images.

The excellent selection of *Pictures and other Passages from Henry James* will save the reader who wishes to revise his estimate of Henry James a good deal of time. Here are spread out, as it were, samples of James's qualities, and in such a variety and in such numbers that nobody ought to fail to come to a final judgement. One does not need to read very long, for instance, to discover that Henry James never got entirely rid of his American accent; or, perhaps, I should call it taste. We read of 'the touch of the air' as 'gloved'; and there occurs this piece of bathos: 'Our friends bent their backs in their gardens and their noses over its symptoms' (Spring's). What classic English writer could commit these errors in serious writing? I know no more than a hundred and thirteen, and they do not count. But Henry James is full of them. They are, in fact, a feature of his style. But of his astonishing subtlety this book is no less well filled with examples and it is, after all, this that we read him for. What matter that his style bumps every now and then as if his mind were driving over a colonial road—for the most part his meaning is translucent, and exquisitely subtle. What I have said before of James, I can repeat now with an even clearer conscience after having read him *in petto*. He stands midway between matter and mind, and on the very tip-top of social culture. There is no mistake about it: James is the best schoolmaster of psychological manners of any novelist that has ever written. This follows from both his equipment and his method. Acutely awake to impressions, he kept himself attentive by never sparing himself any consciousness when in the presence of a personality. He never, as he says, 'economized consciousness'. And what he looked for was only for a moment or two the physical character of his object: the rest of his concern was with its mode of expressing itself. Impressions of expressions —there, I think, you have Henry James; and I leave it to be judged whether our manners to one another would not be improved if we were all as sensitive in both as he was.

KIPLING

The specific quality of Kipling is energetics—work, action, in any form. This is indicated by a thousand signs. His titles mainly refer to action—actions and reactions, traffics and discoveries, the day's work, many inventions. Again, look at the variety of his technical descriptions, all of crafts and trades of one kind or another. Or at the burden of his best-known verses, concerning the 'Wise Lord God, Master of Every Trade', or at the moral of 'Tomlinson'. It is clear that he has taken *au pied de la lettre* the conclusion of Voltaire's *Candide,* that exquisite burlesque of the easy optimism of the talker. '*Il faut cultiver nos jardins*', said Candide. Work without thinking! Kipling's admiration of workmen—particularly of workmen who talk wi' deeficulty—amounts to snobbery. Having himself scarcely ever knocked a nail in a wall, he yet aspires to be taken by every craftsman as a past-master—an old hand at every trade. Among tinkers he would wish to pass as a superannuated tinker; among soldiers as an old soldier; among mechanics as a retired foreman. His snobbery in the presence of the accomplished even includes the accomplishments of animals; among the creatures of the Jungle he is wise old Kaa; elsewhere he is an old dog, a fox, a seal of many summers, a worker-bee, and a score of other things.

This is an admirable ambition, and entitles Kipling to be regarded as the voice of the Demiurgus, who is said to have

created the world while the other gods were talking about
it. His sympathy is with creation. It is, moreover, the natural
reaction of a powerful mind from the windbagism denounced by Carlyle so voluminously. To be able to test
work done, here and now, without waiting for a hypo-
thetical Day of Judgement, is a relief for the practical man
from the burden and doubt of speculation. Kipling is a
pragmatist who asks to be judged by immediate results, the
more immediate the better. For this reason he loves, above
all, machinery and the sea, since neither is amenable to the
sweetest reasoning or will delay their judgement of skill
and workmanship for a moment. 'Ye shall not clear,' he
makes Poseidon say to the 'robust and brass-bound man',
the soul that cannot tell a lie—'except upon the land':

Ye shall not clear by Greekly speech, nor cozen from your path,
The twinkling shoal, the leeward beach, and Hadrian's white-
    lipped wrath.

No, Greekly speech cannot 'put the come-over' on Poseidon;
and hence Kipling awards merits to sailors who pass the
sea's test with flying colours. It is a salutary tonic for idle
dreamers of empty days. Nevertheless it is not the whole
truth; and Kipling pays with many serious defects for his
partiality. His exclusive homage to the doers in life forces
him to cinematize them beyond their own recognition and
certainly beyond their gratitude. Kipling's praise of them,
if they should read it, would make them blush with shame.
His eulogies are laid on with a trowel. He is also most unjust
to men of pure thought, for which he will find the gates of
immortality in our literature shut one day against him.
Being able to 'do' nothing, having no craftwork to show,
the thinkers (worst when they also debate!) are for Kipling
'bandalog'—chattering monkeys, the derision of the practical
Jungle animals, and, of course, the terror-stricken victims
of the great Kaa himself, when he chooses! But Voltaire

did not mean Candide's conclusion to be taken *quite* so literally. Voltaire was one of the fathers of the French Revolution, and it was bandalogging that did it! Besides, the talk of to-day is the task of to-morrow. Not 'Deeds not Words' should be our motto; but 'Words *and* Deeds'— with words first. Kipling would have deeds first and words nowhere; as if the only redemption of work from servility were not in the capacity to talk about it!

It is only the accomplished that Kipling cares about. What is still in process of becoming the embryonic, the promising, the tentative, get no sympathy from him. It is remarked by everybody that his boys talk like men; it may be added that he is so impatient of the slow process of evolution that he makes every created thing to speak in 'man talk'. His 'work without thinking' likewise involves him in acquiescence in authority, authority of any kind. All Kipling's heroes, man and beast, are 'under orders', and are therewith absolved from the responsibility of even intelligent co-operation with their superiors. His conception of duty is the Civil Servant's; and God is merely the Chief of all the departments of the Universe. *He* knows what *He* is about, and we have only to obey and ask no questions. It is clear that Kipling is not Lucifer, but Gabriel; and perhaps not even Gabriel—who was a messenger indeed, but of light! Gabrielism, however, is out of place on earth, where Satan is as likely as God to command obedience. The born workman, such as Kipling loves, doubtless finds nothing better than to do his job without questioning the command he is under; as there are wage-slaves and formerly were serfs and slaves, to whom mere work is satisfaction enough. But we are not beavers or ants to pile up work intelligently yet without intelligence. The ambition to stimulate in wage-slaves is to become, at any cost, at least junior partners in the management of their industry; and with Lucifer we should stimulate in mankind the will to become at least junior partners in the management of the world. But Kipling is a reactionary, philosophically no less than socially. He hates the very thought of rebellion; and the notion of men sitting in a corner to plot in talk some new liberty for themselves strikes him as indecent. For this very reason Shaw and Wells, with all their faults, are better men than Kipling. They are the blind puppies of a new breed, the abecedarians of a new creed. Kipling belongs to the past. He has no more interest than the accomplished fact.

There is a strain of mysticism in Kipling that redeems his work from the vulgarity that otherwise would surely weigh it down to the level of Mr. William Le Queux. Of ideas he has no more than the rest of the magazine writers; but his range of feeling, both upwards and downwards, is far wider than theirs. The mahatma in *Kim* is a sympathetic figure, though all the efforts of the modern theosophists, to whose work as pioneers *Kim* owes its being, go unrecognized by Kipling, and probably inspire him with contempt. He sympathizes with persons, with characters, but not with ideas. Again, his range among the psychic phenomena of personality is wide. He is aware of the abysmal depths of human consciousness. Look at *The Finest Story in the World*, or *The Brushwood Boy*, both excellent short stories and both sympathetic, to say the least, to the speculation of psychic research. Yet Kipling has added nothing, not so much as a 'case', to the study of the undeveloped faculties of man. He is waiting as usual, until the 'chattering' is over. For the rest he is sentimental at bottom and disposed to sweetness rather than to light. The 'Envoi' with which he concludes many of his stories is the old-fashioned moral drawn in sentimental terms. It is the banjo-ditty played when the day's work is over: sweet often, but sedative always.

STENDHAL

Henri Beyle, better known as Stendhal, dying in 1842, prophesied that he would only begin to be generally read in 1880. His forecast was so far false that long before 1880 he was read and admired by Balzac and Taine, read and hated by Sainte-Beuve and Goethe; and was so far true that until about 1880, even the praise of more popular writers (I mean journalists) like Zola, Bourget, Maurice Barrès and André Gide, did not inspire his publishers to large editions. At present, however, there is a cult of 'Beylisme' in France, and every scrap of his writing, memoirs, letters, notebooks, etc., is finding its way into elaborately annotated editions. Two or three causes are responsible for this, though none of them is mentioned in the study of Stendhal by Mr. Lytton Strachey. Nietzsche's homage to Stendhal should be put as the main excitation from the outside of the new cult. To the extent that Nietzsche himself is read and admired, naturally, his admitted sources will be examined— for who would not wish to retrace the path of one's hero in the hope of becoming a hero on one's own? A second cause is the present political condition of France, with its critical hesitation between a new movement forward and a reaction backwards. This is not the place to discuss the state of political thought in France; but the hint of Mr. John Eglinton that the French Revolution marked 'the end of the Christian era' should prepare us to realize the still doubtful issue of what should come after that event. Is France, having closed one epoch, to open another, the post-domini; or, in fearful panic, to crawl back to a mere A.D.? That is the question now being put everywhere, though nowhere, I think, with the foregoing bluntness. Stendhal, in my judgement, belongs definitely to the post-domini era; and for this reason is now become a rallying-point for progress. Nor does it refute me to point out that French reactionaries like Bourget also appeal to him; for reactionaries are always very stupid or very clever. Nietzsche's admiration for Stendhal was not, however, a misunderstanding, but, if not, how comes M. Bourget, or even M. Barrès, to praise Stendhal? Have they misunderstood? But no, M. Barrès says that Stendhal is 'a collector of fine energies', which is somewhere near the truth. The truth itself, however, is that Stendhal substituted energy for 'goodness' as the criterion of virtue. And here, I am sure, M. Barrès would not agree with him.

But do my readers—for, after all, who is M. Barrès to us? Assuming that the character of Christian civilization is the elevation of 'goodness', with or without strength, as the ideal—is it permissible to eliminate the question of 'goodness' and to measure virtue in energy only? From this point of view, what is to be sought and admired in man is primarily his energy, his power, represented by his will to assert himself; and only of secondary consideration is the direction or object of his energy. It will be seen that in adopting this code we should find our preferences consorting with strange companies—criminals, for instance, provided they did not suffer remorse, and people of that type. Are we prepared for it? Firstly, the doctrine assumes an apathy requiring to be whipped into movement. France is fatigued, France is asleep, France needs to be roused— hence Stendhal is the whip of France. Secondly, I hate a universal commandment that is not at the same time natural to everybody. Are we all to be always storing energy quantitatively and none of us to be refining what we have? Surely the double process might go on simultaneously: and that, I hope, will be the case. Stendhal, I may add, failed exemplarily. He made his style powerful (he modelled it, in fact, on the Code Napoléon), but nobody can say he made it beautiful. Of beauty none of us need be afraid; but energy without beauty is not post-domini, but B.C.

MR. G. K. CHESTERTON

It is too late to expect Mr. G. K. Chesterton to change his style, or, rather, to adapt it to his subject; so it must be said, *tout simplement*, that the style of *The Crimes of England* is a deplorable misfit. In the tradition of literature there is an established rule that the matter and manner must be somehow in harmony; and, moreover, the particular harmonies are by this time pretty well established. For instance, you would not expect to find an epic in limerick-meter; nor would you expect to find puns in a funeral oration. Mr. G. K. Chesterton has, however, one manner (I am speaking of his prose only), which he applies to every matter. Let the subject be naturally cheerful, fanciful, serious, or tragic, the same style may confidently be looked for from him—and consequently the same result will be achieved. As an exhibition of Mr. Chesterton's miraculous cleverness, Mr. Chesterton's almost fanatical earnestness, Mr. Chesterton's knowledge and insight, *The Crimes of England* is one of his two best works; but as an *exposé* of the crimes of England or, for the matter of that, of Germany either, it is unconvincing. The truth of what Mr. Chesterton says is the last thing readers think about. So dazzled are we by the verbal sparklings of Mr. Chesterton's wit, that it is as if we were trying to read by the light of fireworks: we can read nothing for the explosions and the coloured spectacles. Look, for example, at this passage, which is typical:

Cobbett was defeated because the English people was defeated. After the frame-breaking riots, men, as men, were beaten; and machines, as machines, had beaten them. Peterloo was as much the defeat of the English as Waterloo was the defeat of the French. Ireland did not get Home Rule because England did not get it. Cobbett would not forcibly incorporate Ireland, least of all the corpse of Ireland.

Read one after the other in the ordinary way, they stun the mind like a series of shocks; no meaning can survive them. And considered sentence by sentence they scarcely repay the trouble.

Upon some fantastic subject such an intrusion of the oddities of the writer is no intrusion at all. Provided that the whole subject is one for cleverness, brilliance, and literary fun, Mr. Chesterton's style is made in heaven to suit it. But in a matter by no means of Mr. Chesterton's invention—namely, the War—and one in which the oddest of us ought to feel and act and think like a citizen of the world, the apparition of Mr. Chesterton in all his idiosyncrasies is very nearly an impertinence. Matthew Arnold used to say that the business of the critic is to get himself out of the way of the author he wishes to present. However that may be—for it is not the whole truth—the business of anybody who writes on public affairs at a time when they are really public is to write as if he were a scribe simply, and the public dictating: 'the hearts of all consenting to the voice of one'. It was in this 'common' style (as elevated, however, as the writer could rise in the 'common' mind) that Demosthenes and Lincoln delivered their orations, and Swift transcribed his 'Conduct of the Allies'. True, the style still remained individual, unique; but it was, nevertheless, the style in which its readers would wish themselves to write if they could. Save for inevitable refraction, the subject shone so clearly through it that the actual writer might easily have been overlooked—as he had overlooked himself while writing. Nobody, however, can forget in reading *The Crimes of England* that it is

Mr. G. K. Chesterton and nobody else who is writing. His inversions and antitheses and paradoxes betray his presence as clearly and as improperly as the egoistic interludes of Mr. Bernard Shaw. Both, therefore, may profess as sincerely as they please that they write for England; but England writes for herself in neither of them.

I must except from these comments the dedicatory letter to 'Professor Whirlwind', and the concluding chapter describing the Battle of the Marne. In the former Mr. Chesterton has a particular person to address, and in the latter a dramatic historic episode to describe. In the one he writes with restraint, powerfully, and yet persuasively; in the other his foot is on his native heath of vivid description, and the result is admirable. Long after his works have followed him, his letters will remain as examples of written debate.

Mr. G. K. Chesterton will never write a better book than his *Charles Dickens;* but what on earth the public will make of it I cannot guess. Without being in the least sophistical, Mr. Chesterton appears as a master of sophistry. Without wishing to confuse any issues, Mr. Chesterton confuses all issues. Wishing to say nothing but the simple and the true, he is the most complex and paradoxical writer our language has produced. In some ways, indeed, Mr. Chesterton, though a critic of our days, is its most complete incarnation; all styles are to be found in him save any style; all ideas save any idea; all points of view save any point of view. A study of Mr. G. K. Chesterton would dispense us from the necessity of considering any of his contemporaries.

THE MARKS OF MR. WELLS

Hitherto in his novels Mr. Wells has written of his contemporaries under thinly disguised names. In *Boon*, purporting to be the work of Mr. 'Reginald Bliss', he reverses the method, and under a thin disguise discusses his contemporaries under their proper names. Such an affectation of anonymity is childish. It is as bad as Mr. Shaw referring mysteriously to the author of *Fanny's First Play*. It is like amateur conjuring, at which we are expected to pretend to be mystified. And what Mr. Wells obtains in the way of freedom by the transparent disguise I cannot gather. Were not his descriptions of living people in *Ann Veronica*, for example, free enough? Does he want still more licence than he has already taken? If it were so, I for one should be happy to give it him; but in *Boon* his comments on his contemporaries are milder than those he has published under his own name. I can only conclude that he has been playing floor-games so long that he is now playing with his public. That Mr. Wells, and not Mr. 'Reginald Bliss', is the author of this book is even more apparent in the text than in the arch Introduction. Mr. Wells's accidental prejudices, preferences, and tricks recur throughout with the regularity of the footprints of a buffalo on a tract of shining mud. There are envious gibes at the Academic Committee, of which Mr. Wells is *not* a member. There are the famous dots. . . . The writer defends the formlessness of such novels as Mr. Wells writes against the form of the novels of Mr. Henry James. He never mentions the name of Mr. Wells, but he is always talking of him as if he were perpetually apologizing for his existence. He pleads for severe thought and discussion and shows himself incapable of either. Finally he sinks exhausted in a puddle of self-depreciation which he mistakes for good will. If

H

these are not the marks of Mr. Wells may I be fillipped with a three-man beetle.

In his Introduction Mr. Wells says: 'I will confess I have not read the book through'. With much more truth I can boast the same confession, and probably in full company. Nobody, indeed, who has any respect for his time and mind will fail to skip. One or two illustrations of the foregoing observations, however, have caught my eye, and here they are. In a passably witty phrase Mr. Wells describes Mr. Shaw as an 'intellectual jackdaw' in imitation of Mr. Shaw's own description of himself as 'a crow that has followed many ploughs'—which is better! But when he continues that Mr. Shaw's 'stuff is too incoherent and recklessly positive ever to be systematically answered', then Mr. Wells is most perfectly describing himself. Contrast, however, his description of this quality of formlessness when he thinks he perceives it in Mr. Shaw with his account of it when he sees it in Mr. Wells. Mr. Shaw is incoherence; but Mr. Boon (that is Mr. Wells) is 'one of those people who will *not* photograph: so much of him is movement, gesture, expression, atmosphere and colour, and so little of him is form'. What, in short, is incoherence in Mr. Shaw is movement, gesture, etc., in Mr. Wells! From a man who has never 'thought' in his life, this challenge is something amusing: 'Are there no men to think at least as earnestly as one climbs a mountain and to write with their uttermost pride?' There are, Mr. Wells, there are—but they are your antipodes and naturally your aversion. You describe them, in fact, as 'semi-mineral minds' (why not marble or golden?) without movement, gesture, and all the rest of the virtues! (including emoluments and advertisement?). As an example of his humour—almost American in its form—take this: 'Ordinary people snuggle up to God as a lost leveret in a freezing wilderness might snuggle up to

a Siberian tiger'. A more polished thrust is this: 'Mr.
Norman Angell advertises himself in a small magazine and
resents any other work for peace as though it were an
infringement of his copyright'. Finally, as I say, he collapses
in a slop of sentiment. On the last page we are told that 'it
does not matter how individually feeble we writers and
disseminators are; we have to hunt the Wild Asses; as the
feeblest puppy has to bark at cats and burglars'. What a
scale of imagination for an intellectual hunter! But the
enemies of Truth and Beauty and Right are not mere
cats and burglars; and neither puppies nor even full-
grown dogs will scare them away: they are devils and
demons.

Only as a morbid study would I comment here upon
Mr. Wells's new novel, *The Research Magnificent*. As a novel
simply it is beneath notice. We may see, indeed, in Mr.
Wells's recent work the *reductio ad absurdum* of his anarchic
theories of this literary form. Listen to him upon Mr. Henry
James. 'James', he says, 'has never discovered that a novel
isn't a picture. He wants a novel to be simply and completely
done. He wants it to have a unity; he demands homogeneity. . . . But if the novel is to follow life it must be
various and discursive.' Who demanded that the novel
should 'follow' life? No artist, it is certain. 'Leading' life
is more the way of the creator. And, again, who but
Mr. Wells disputes Mr. James's claim that a novel must be
a unity and have homogeneity? The effect of Mr. Wells's
theories is to be seen in contrast with the effects Mr. James
produces. In the latter the illusion of life is preserved, but
of life in selected aspects designed to exhibit a single mood
or a single character. But in the former everything sprawls
like the items in a daily paper. String on a thin running
motive the contents of any issue of the *Times* from 'Births,
Deaths, and Marriages' to 'Property Sales', and the result

is one of Mr. Wells's recent novels. And twopence is less than six shillings!

The morbid interest, however, is not confined to the form, it includes the leading characters of Mr. Wells's latest novels. I could believe that he was metamorphosed in Russia and has become a Russian, so similar are now his heroes to the painfully crucified protagonists of Russian literature. The 'harmony of will and deed' is in Mr. Wells's heroes a discord ever growing more depressing. They start off with dreams which only supermen could realize, and find, after a chapter or two, that their author has equipped them with the character of moral imbeciles. What end is possible but suicide or subsidence into some corner of life? That such characters *appeared* to be common a year or two ago is an admission I make to Mr. Wells. There were, indeed, scores of young men in the pre-War days whose imagination stretched its neck miles beyond their forefeet. But it was an appearance only, as the War proved. Mr. Wells presumably took an interest in the War and, professionally, in its reactions upon psychology. Where now, except in concealed literary circles, does he find his Benhams? And if there be any such, I doubt whether the stumbling block is always sex. Sex, for Mr. Wells's later heroes, is the *pons asinorum* upon which they always come to grief. This is not the case with his Russian peers, who usually contrive a greater trial than physical sex. In this respect, therefore, Mr. Wells is worse than the Russians. However, it is all symptomatic, I dare say; and Mr. Wells is the infant of the passing age. These novels will pass with it.

Mr. Wells's *Passionate Friends* is not a masterly work in any sense of the word, but, on the contrary, as loose and incontinent a production, both in style and ideas, as could well be produced by an habitual writer. Usually, as is well

known, an author becomes more real, defined, and concrete
as his discipline of thought and writing invigorates his
mind. Ruskin, for example, who began as a windbag,
ended by nearly writing perfect good sense; in time he
would have written, perhaps, as simply as Swift wrote, or
as passionately to the point as Demosthenes spoke. With
Mr. Wells, however, the case is just the reverse. He began
by writing of definite persons, things, and ideas, and he is
now writing indefinitely of anything. In fact, he appears to
suppose that indefiniteness is a virtue, a quality characteristic
of the best intelligence. To obliterate the natural or acquired
distinctions between the sexes, for instance, is for him a
kind of duty to civilization. When his heroine, the Lady
Mary, talks of living her own life and belonging to herself,
not only does the fool hero, Stephen, assent to her claim
to these male privileges, but Mr. Wells pleads for the view
with an almost personal appeal. But such chatter on the
part of a woman like Mary, incapable of supporting herself
for a day, is chatter and nothing more; and if Stephen were
not the 'complementary male' spoken of by Dr. Almroth
Wright, he would have either laughed at her or turned and
left her. That, I hope and believe, is what young men are
to-day doing with the apes of the wives of Ibsen's and
Shaw's eunuchs and baby-husbands. But just as Mr. Wells
is no longer able to discriminate between a man and a
woman, and would have it that a woman can possibly be
as 'free' as a man, so, I find, he is no longer able to discriminate between economic and spiritual affairs, between
democracy and aristocracy, between one form of government and another, between Socialism and aimless amiable
Social Reform. On all these subjects, in the course of inter-
minable digressions, Mr. Wells exfoliates to marvel, but he
never by any chance drops a seed. I did not note in my reading a single observation fit to be placed at the head of an
essay or demanding a moment's reflection to open it. This,

which would be no defect if the story were continuous, is a damning defect in a story deliberately interrupted to admit reflections and observations. The book, as my readers will gather, irritated me. It did more, it disgusted me. There is not a sign of passion (which is intelligent single-mindedness) in the *Passionate Friends* from beginning to end. What Mr. Wells calls passion is nothing but lust. All the chief characters are as promiscuous as they can hang together. There is neither charm nor virtue in one of them.

Mr. Wells's lecture to the Royal Institution—under the title *The Discovery of the Future*—I have read again, for the purpose of testing its durability as an idea. Alas, it has not worn well at all. The assumption made by Mr. Wells that science was providing materials for prophecy unknowable by the antique sages has proved to be without foundation, as far, at least, as the essentials of humanity are concerned. That Mr. Wells was himself a brilliant prophet in the region of mechanics, I readily admit. A score, nay, a thousand engineers with his gift of words would produce you forecasts of the probable inventions of the next fifty years. But what is mechanics to the soul of man? In a peroration—very shabby in the cold dawn after these years—Mr. Wells appears to have confused them as he confuses still material with spiritual progress: 'All this world', he declaims, 'is heavy with the promise of greater things, and a day will come, one day in the unending succession of days, when beings, beings who are now latent in our thoughts and hidden in our loins, shall stand upon this earth as one stands upon a footstool, and shall laugh and reach out their hands amid the stars'. Loud applause from the gallery in which I do not join. We are not amused.

Not, believe me, that I reject the optimism which inspires it as ridiculous, but because I know now that such optimism is a light and easy mood, too flimsy to afford a base for the task it sets itself. To begin reaching out hands to the stars, there is necessary something more than aeroplanes, something more, indeed, than any machine or mechanical power ever to be invented: the development of the latent powers of the mind. But mechanical progress, in which Mr. Wells superseded Jules Verne as a popular prophet, is almost, if not quite, a substitute for, and certainly a diversion from, intellectual progress. So, likewise, I believe, is the eugenic progress Mr. Wells appeared to have in mind. The Superman—if I may be sententious for a moment—will not be born of woman, but of man.

SHAW AND REALITY

At a recent Times Book Club meeting, Mr. Temple Thurston, the novelist, made a commendable excursion into philosophy. He began by some silly verbal paradoxes (another fossil remain of the Eighteen-Nineties) concerning the identity of realism and sentiment, but clarified himself as he proceeded and finally arrived at something like sense. There must be, he affirmed, some ultimate intention in the conduct of the world, and hence some good reason for our being here. Reality consists in the appreciation of this purpose, and art in its illumination. Mr. Thurston may, of course, be challenged for the proofs of his faith; but, if he is wise, he will offer none at present. In fact, intellectually, we are honourably bound to agnosticism. But this does not make impossible certain hopeful guesses or imaginative hypotheses, one of which is this: that in time we shall find a reason for everything. I believe that we are not so far off the discovery of a few more 'reasons' as materialists imagine.

On the supposition—purely supposition, note—that there is an 'intention' in the conduct of the world, an 'intention', discoverable by and, in the long run, agreeable to, human reason—of which 'intention', moreover, we and our reason are part—a modified doctrine of the absolute in matters of ethics would certainly be necessary. And without such a doctrine anarchism, it appears to me, is inevitable. At one time in his inconsistent career Mr. Shaw turned philosopher and predicated as the 'intention' of the world the creation of brains. 'The Universe', he said, 'is aiming at its darling object, brains.' This hypothesis of an end, as was pointed out, required of Mr. Shaw that he should classify all acts accordingly. Those that led to the development of brains were good, those that militated against brains were bad. But in his recent article on the Bishop of Kensington Mr. Shaw seems to have relapsed into anarchism; for he therein professed to believe that the moral and the immoral are merely matters of personal opinion. If the good, the right, the moral, and their opposites are merely matters of opinion, it follows that there is no known criterion in the form of a universal 'intention' by which to classify them. But once upon a time Mr. Shaw said there was! To which Mr. Shaw shall we appeal? My own view is that in predicating 'brains' as the 'intention' of the universe Mr. Shaw was too impatient of the travail of soul necessary to win the right to predicate any particular end at all. It is not everybody whose faith has any value: much faith evaporates, even in the process of gaining disciples. How many saviours have died disillusioned! Mr. Shaw has apparently lived to be disillusioned. I am not, however, defending the Bishop of Kensington. He is with the ninety and nine sheep of the Church who have never gone astray—and consequently may at any time!

Mr. Shaw's early novel, *An Unsocial Socialist,* has just been republished. It was either of this or of another of Mr. Shaw's novels of the same period that Stevenson said something flattering. Stevenson might, for he was no critic; but the truth is that Mr. Shaw had not even the making of a novelist in him. His observation, of course, is amazing, but it is not in the least penetrating. I mean that it never goes deeper than the level of his subjects' own knowledge. Whatsoever secrets a man keeps from himself—and that a profound observer would divine—are hidden from Mr. Shaw as well. He is level with the brain, but never as deep as the heart. But this should have decided him, if he wanted to write stories, to write short stories only. A long story all on the level of ratiocination is wearisome; and *An Unsocial Socialist* proves it. Here we have no crises, except those of farce or mere contretemps; nor is there any real joy. The story, characters and all, rattles along like a conversazione of the Fabian Society. One knows that no great issues are at stake. As a variant of *Dolly Dialogues,* in brief witty episodes, the same story would have been amusing and, on its level, instructive. The necessary variety would have spared us the boredom of the continuous hero. Mr. Shaw learnt wisdom early enough to drop novels for plays. It is a pity his plays are not all one-act curtain raisers; for his creative inspiration is never longer than a happy quarter of an hour.

Mr. Shaw's defence of his *Androcles and the Lion* against the attacks of the 'divines' does not strike me as very effective. Indeed, long after his buzzing brilliance is out of my ears, I find it hard to sum up what he has said. Is there any 'gist' in Shaw at all or ever? Does he not always say everything, and therefore nothing? It is absurd for him to go on repeating that an honest Christian would infallibly find himself in prison. He knows that such talk is cant. Before the *New Statesman* appeared, Mr. Shaw said in an interview that he should consider himself lucky if the staff escaped prison (prison again) for a couple of issues. There have been twenty-six up to date; Mr. Shaw, I believe, has written in most of them; he is not only still out of prison, but he and

his staff are well on the way to be knighted. Again, he
pretends to find the world shocking, and divines in general
a set of self-deluded scoundrels. But his language is much
stronger than his feelings: in short, it is rhetoric. For instance,
in his reply to the Rev. Morgan Gibbon, of whom, *ex
hypothesi*, he thinks ill, neither the general reader, nor, I dare
wager, the Rev. Morgan Gibbon himself, can discover anything offensive. Theoretically Mr. Shaw is in a state of
manly indignation; actually he is damned amiable. It is not
true, either, that Mr. Shaw does not 'sneer' or that when he
despises a thing he 'insults it in the most unmistakably direct
terms'. I remember nothing that he has insulted in his life;
and sneering is surely only fault-finding without fault-
feeling. On partial consideration—for I confess that Mr.
Shaw is still an enigma—I should summarize his whole
doctrine as: 'Be brilliant or bust'. If anybody cared to change
'or' into 'and', I should not dispute the difference.

The idea has probably struck us all at one time or another
to attempt to read the New Testament as if it had made its
first appearance yesterday. But it is impossible to read the
Bible with a fresh mind, for we have not a fresh mind to
bring to it. We can no more read the Testaments as if we
had never read them before than we can look at ourselves
in the glass as if we were newly introduced. When we attempt
the task we find that we cannot make head or tail of the
narrative. For the industry, almost antlike in its dull pertin-
acity, of Mr. Shaw's effort to extract a coherent and rational
story out of the Gospels I have what must, I suppose, be
called admiration. It is a feat of human endurance. But as
for serving any purpose beyond confirming the general
opinion that such attempts are bound to fail, I see no value
in Mr. Shaw's Preface (*Androcles and the Lion*).

It is well known that everybody finds in the Bible what he
looks for. Such a ragbag as both Testaments are of fragments

of history, fragments of mysticism, fragments of ethics, fragments of symbology, of poetry, of religion, of politics and of personal biography, we need not wonder that everybody can find a scrap in them to suit him. But when it comes to making a pattern of the whole, or to piecing the fragments of the jigsaw puzzle to form a single picture, nobody has ever succeeded in it and nobody ever will. It would be just as easy to construct a story out of the chance collection of the British Museum as to construct a story out of the New Testament; for the New Testament *is* a museum, and the principles that governed its collection were quite as fortuitous as those that govern the collection of any other museum. What happens when anybody sets about the impossible task is, in the first place, an arbitrary selection of a point of view; and, in the second place, an arbitrary rejection or interpretation of everything that does not fit into it. Thus one man will set out with the intention of proving the hero of the Gospels to have been a Dionysian. There are plenty of texts to support his view, and by a judicious parallelism of passages between the Bible and the Dionysian writers he can appear to establish his case—but only by tacitly suppressing as many equally authentic texts that bear a precisely contrary meaning. Another man will wish to show that Jesus was first and foremost a Jewish religious reformer. Still another represents Him as a man of sorrows, while a different school holds Him to have been a child of joy. And each of these views is firmly based upon a selection of texts—and upon the suppression of the rest. Mr. Shaw is no exception to the hitherto unbroken rule of procedure. Setting out with the fixed intention of reading the Gospels impartially, he finds himself (or we find him) first selecting his point of view and next selecting or rejecting among the texts to fit it. What his selected point of view is his readers might have guessed before ever they saw it set to work. It is that Jesus was an early forerunner of the modern founder of the

Fabian Society—a man, that is, uncommonly like Mr. Shaw himself in his virtues, but with weaknesses which his successful disciple has been too wise to share. The founder of Christianity, in short, turns out to have been Mr. Shaw in an earlier imperfect incarnation, and His doctrine to have been an intelligent anticipation of Fabianism. All this, as I say, was to be expected from Mr. Shaw's engagement in the impossible task of making a unity of the New Testament. It was doubly to be expected from Mr. Shaw's obstinate obsession that the meaning of history is Fabianism.

What is new in Mr. Shaw's Preface is not his view of the New Testament, but the evidence of his fear of Mr. G. K. Chesterton. This comes out vividly in several passages that I shall quote, and in a philosophic admission that made me open my eyes. The quotations are as follows:

We have always had a curious feeling that, though we crucified Christ on a stick, He somehow managed to get hold of the right end of it.

Paul's natural hatred of the Teacher for whom Sin and Death had no terrors turned into a wild personal worship of Him which has the gentleness of a beautiful thing seen in a false light.

. . . will rise again in golden beauty amidst a great burst of sunshine and bird-music.

These passages are not Mr. Shaw, but Mr. Shaw writing to conciliate Mr. Chesterton. And the observation is supported by the strange doctrine that Mr. Shaw has borrowed from Mr. Chesterton concerning the subjectivity of truth, and hence of the credibility of miracles. Some years ago a debate took place between these two friendly parties in which the point turned upon the credibility of the miracle of the liquefaction of the blood of St. Januarius. Mr. Chesterton contended that the evidence for the fact of the miracle was

sufficient for belief; and Mr. Shaw, I remember, not only
denied that it was sufficient, but challenged Mr. Chesterton
to assert that the miracle was a fact. Since that day a change
seems to have taken place, for Mr. Shaw now agrees that
'there is as much evidence that the miracles occurred as that
the battle of Waterloo occurred'. It is enough to say upon
this point that nobody can believe it, and that nobody does.
The less serious implication is that Mr. Shaw has succumbed
to Mr. Chesterton; and the more serious implication is that
he has become a romantic. If, as he now says, belief is not
dependent upon evidence and reason, but upon fashion and
the prevailing prejudices, then all that can be asserted of
any man's belief is that the only certain truth about it is
that he believes it. Its truth or falsity is another thing altogether; and a thing apparently which there is no means of
settling. Whether, for example, the blood of St. Januarius
liquefies annually, or whether the battle of Waterloo was
ever fought, you will believe or not believe according to
the prevailing fashion. Under the influence of the Catholic
Church you will believe the one on as good evidence and
with as good reason as, under the influence of historical
research, you will believe the other. Both are equally matters
of taste, and hence of belief or of disbelief according to the
accepted standards of the day. To admit such 'reasoning' is,
however, to fly in the face of reason, which, while distin-
guishing between beliefs founded upon fashions and beliefs
founded upon fact, denies that the same class of facts support
the miracle as support the reality of Waterloo. We can
never have established for us, by the same means that the
fact of Waterloo is established for us, the fact of the St.
Januarius miracle; and the means by which Waterloo is
established are the very means by which St. Januarius is
disestablished. Over and above this objection there is the
objection that if we abandon the belief in the objectivity
of truth, leaving nothing but subjective truth or truth

determined by our will and no longer by our total judgement, not only has objective truth no meaning, but the
subjective truth that is left has no value. What is it to us that
men should give us a catalogue of their beliefs if their beliefs
are professedly idiosyncrasies, exempt even from the pretence
of being based upon truths for everybody? It would require
a psychopathic doctor to become interested in such auto-
biographies, and their value would then be as symptoms
of a state of mind rather than as affirmations of a state of
reality. In conceding to Mr. Chesterton's Catholicism the
equal value of the evidence for miracles and for Waterloo,
Mr. Shaw has really sold the pass of truth. He has become
a romantic to whom the criterion of truth is the intensity
of conviction. Mr. Shaw has been in strange company, but
I never expected to see him among the romantics.

SOREL, MARX, AND THE DRAMA

Sorel's *Reflections on Violence* is one of the few works upon
Socialism that can be, and deserves to be, read by the non-
professional student. Socialist authors for the most part are
for Socialist readers exclusively. They are usually economic
dissenting parsons addressing a conventicle of the already
saved in language of a sectarian circumscription. Occasionally, however, one of them breaks loose from the sect and
the language of the sect, and addresses the world in the
language of the world. And Sorel is one of these. Regarding
his thesis that a 'myth' is necessary to the creation of a revolutionary movement, and that in particular the 'myth' of
the General Strike is indispensable to the modern proletarian
movement, I am not convinced, nor is it necessary that any
man should be. It is rather poetry than a political idea, and
belongs to the same order of thought as the Republicanism
of Plato. But there is no doubt in my mind that the idea is

of value on that very account. What has been lacking in
Socialism—with the exception of Marx's *Capital,* in which
the tremendous historical tragedy of capitalism is recorded—
is sublimity, the sense of the grand. Sorel's contribution of a
'myth' to the movement is therefore of the nature of art;
it lifts the commonplace into the ideal world by deepening
its significance. 'Socialists', he says, 'must be convinced that
the work to which they are devoting themselves is a serious,
formidable, and sublime work; it is only on this condition
that they will be able to bear the innumerable sacrifices
imposed on them by a propaganda that can procure them
neither honours, profits, nor even immediate intellectual
satisfaction.' Even if the only result of the idea of the General
Strike is to make the Socialist conception more heroic, it
should on that account alone be looked upon as having an
incalculable value.

Over against this view of Socialism as something tremendous, sublime, heroic, and hence worthy of the unrewarded
devotion of a lifetime, may be set the views of the merely
political Socialists who look for results, both to their own
advantage and to the advantage of the movement, here and
now. Sorel is properly critical of the character of such men.
Of the leaders, for example, he says that they have preserved
the Marxist vocabulary while allowing themselves to become
completely estranged from the thought of Marx. They talk
of revolution when all the time they mean evolution. And
seldom without some personal object either. 'The leaders
who foster this sweet illusion (that of immediate reform by
political action) see the situation from quite another point
of view than that of their followers; the present social
organization revolts them just in so far as it creates obstacles
to their ambition; they are less shocked by the existence of
the classes than by their own inability to attain to the posi-
tions already reached by older men; and when they have

penetrated far enough into the sanctuaries of the State, into drawing-rooms and places of amusement, they cease, as a rule, to be revolutionary and speak learnedly of "evolution".' The violence of a proletarian movement, when it is spontaneous, is incalculable: there is no telling to what lengths it might go. But not only calculability is necessary, but control of the movement as well, if the leaders are to be able to dispose of it to their own advantage. For this reason, not only is violence denounced, but measures to nip it, even before it is in the bud, are taken by working class leaders who themselves aspire to belong to the middle classes. The organization of the proletariat in political Trade Unions under a centralized political control, and their diversion from economic to political methods, are plainly dictated by the nature of the problem; and these, as we know, are carried out so effectively that in England the Trade Union leaders, by the power they exercise, are the greatest obstacles to Socialism that exist. From this it may come about that the social revolution of which these leaders have a political vision may end in nothing better than the Servile State. It is hard, indeed, to foresee any other consequence from it. 'It is even possible', says Sorel, 'that, since the transmission of authority operates nowadays almost mechanically, thanks to the new resources at the disposal of the Parliamentary system, and since the proletariat would be thoroughly well organized under the official Trade Unions, we should see the social revolution culminate in a wonderful system of slavery.'

Sorel claims to be the true disciple of Marx, but much to the amusement, it appears, of present-day Marxists. The latter, however, are certainly wrong, for the relation between Marx and Sorel is that of the draughtsman of the plot of the Capitalist tragedy to the artist who concentrates upon the dénouement. Marx unfolded the series of Acts commencing with the birth of the wage-slave, and concluding with the

death of the villain of the piece, namely, Capitalism, at the
hands of its victim. Sorel, on the other hand, chose for his
lesser drama the tragical moment of the climax in the
General Strike. Both, however, had the same conception
of the secular tragedy; but Marx supplied the whole framework, while Sorel worked out the conclusion only. Marx,
it is certain, would no more have repudiated Sorel than
Sorel has repudiated Marx. The difficulty with modern
Marxists is, as Sorel has said, that they have lost their Master's
grand conception of the real nature of the Capitalist tragedy.
They employ his terms, but whittled down to the size of a
paltry movement of a few years. It is as if Milton's epic of
the Loss and Regaining of Paradise should become the text-
book of earnest Plymouth brethren who might continue
to employ Milton's phraseology, but with their mind upon
their parish pump, or, as Ben Jonson said, hearing of Helen
of Troy, but thinking all the time of Elinor Rumming. To
such minds the very notion of the rise and fall of Capitalism,
as representing a tragedy in the history of Mankind, is
romantic and ridiculous. Nothing spiritual do they observe
in it; nor do they climb to the vision of the Proletariat and
the Capitalist as grandiose protagonists in a play lasting over
many centuries. The impatient little creatures want something done at once: they want, in fact, a cinema for an
evening rather than a tragedy for a thousand years.

FALSE MYSTICS

I believe I was the first critic to dispute the claims of Maeterlinck to the title of Mystic. So many of our contemporary
critics are ill-read or not at all read in mystical literature that
they are prepared to accede to anybody's claim to mysticism
provided the vocabulary of the text is bedizened with
mystical terms. But mysticism, if it means anything, means

I

immediacy of knowledge as distinct from mediacy, or knowledge through a medium. It connotes, comparatively, knowledge at first hand as against knowledge at second hand; and second hand here includes knowledge by reasoning, by observation, by deduction, by, in fact, every progressive method known. For example, if the subject should be the survival of the soul after bodily death the psychic researcher may possibly establish the fact by observation and experiment in course of time. I say may, though I do not believe he will. The mystic, on the other hand, *knows* the fact, and proves his knowledge not only by acting upon it, but by being unable to act as if he did not know it! A little reflection will show that the negative test is here of far more importance than the positive. Any of us, blind worms that we are, may hold, for instance, that honesty is the best policy, and act upon the assumption ninety-nine times out of a hundred; but the hundredth will find our faith shaking, because our assumption, after all, is not knowledge immediate of the fact, but knowledge mediate. Now Maeterlinck undoubtedly owed his world-wide sales to the belief he inspired in his readers that he knew in this immediate way much more than the rest of mankind. He was a 'seer', a 'sage', an 'initiate', a 'mystic'.

Analysing his affirmations, however, I long ago discovered them to fall into two categories: guesses and vague deductions. Nowhere in his work did I discover an affirmation by which he himself was prepared to live or die. And now, at last, we have his confession of complete ignorance. In *Our Eternity*, an enlarged version of his recent essay on death, M. Maeterlinck confides to us that he has really been groping about like all the rest of us among psychical researchers, theosophical and spiritualistic and mystical literature, with no other instrument of knowledge than an ordinary ratiocinative brain. And he arrives at the conclusion that we must all be sceptics, though to make agnosticism tolerable to his followers he adds a little of the coloured water of hope and fancy. Well, the truth about Maeterlinck is out at last.

TO-DAY AND TO-MORROW
WHO IS RESPONSIBLE?

The only question on which there is now any disagreement among the competent is the question of responsibility: which of the four parties to current literature is the major criminal—the author, the publisher, the reviewer, or the reader. Against all four there is an active prosecution, less active, however, in the case of the two parties that could really be brought to book. For of readers it is useless to complain: they are as God made them; the best writers have usually the greatest cause to hate them. And of authors similarly I find it hard to make a reasonable complaint. Dependent as they are upon some publishers for appearing in print at all, and then upon some reviewer for the prestige they acquire, they are as completely in the hands of these two as land is in the hands of a farmer. Practically, there exist at any time authors of every degree of possible excellence save genius; and it is not altogether their fault, and still less the fault of the reading public, if the worse and not the better are selected for publication. The real culprits, in fact— certainly the culprits most accessible to exemplary punishment—are the publishers and the reviewers; and though both of these have been blamed, neither have been blamed nearly enough, or as if they were what they are—responsible for the condition of modern literature.

My most general opinion, perhaps, of the condition of modern English literature is this: that as good writers exist potentially to-day as at any time, save the greatest in our history, but that our critics are, without exaggeration, the worst ever known in any world of letters. I do not complain, let it be noted, that our critics do not praise enough: they praise far too much. Nor do I complain that there is not blame enough distributed by the critics of the Press. Up and down there is plenty of it. The real charge to be brought against the dispensers of censure and encomium is that they distribute these precious wares with no respect for the established laws of literature: in short, their criticism is ignorant. Now, say what you like about the stimulus of praise, its value to a sincere writer is nil when he knows that its author simply pours it out by the bucketful. And the same applies to blame when it is distributed by no discernible principle. What I should like to see is reasons given for every judgement. When the judge delivers sentence it should be after a summing-up of the evidence actually before both court and jury; and his principles of judgement should be the established principles of the world's literature. This may seem a Utopian demand, but actually it is no more difficult in the case of literature than in the case of law. To many of the law's best judgements, very few juries could come of their own accord, and certainly never by the way taken by the judges themselves; nevertheless, when delivered and with evidence accompanying them, these best judgements commend themselves to the common sense, even of the average jury. Similarly, I believe that any average body of readers could be brought to appreciate the justness of every sound literary judgement, provided they could be induced to follow the evidence. The unjustness of certain judgements likewise might as easily be brought home to them. I appeal for a more careful reading and for a more careful evidence in every case, and for such evidence as an honest though plain man cannot reject.

Readers occasionally find fault with critics (as I do myself) for apparently having no literary policy—as if you only had to sit down and imagine a policy and then proceed to expound it. But a policy is not arrived at in that way. That way lies idiosyncrasy. To formulate a true policy, two things are required—first, a good standard, and, secondly, a perceptible drift and tendency in one's age. While claiming to possess good standards, our age is for the present too distracted and puzzled to have any particular tendency. Our writers are rotating very busily on their axles, and some, even, set off for somewhere; but who can say that so many as a school are going in the same direction? What, in fact, is *the* literary tendency of the age? Mr. Gosse has made a shot at an answer by defining it as 'the increased study of life in its exhibitions of energy'; and high marks should be given him, for his formula covers a good many of the phenomena. But, on the other hand, it does not cover all, nor the most significant, of existing literary phenomena. I do not observe, for instance, much study of energetics in current novels and plays—where, presumably, it should appear most clearly. On the contrary, our novels and plays are concerned with very supine people as a rule, as remote from exhibitions of astonishing energy as from ideals of any kind. In verse, perhaps, Mr. Gosse's case is a little stronger; for Mr. Masefield undoubtedly preaches energetics and, quite as undoubtedly, is somewhat of a fashion. But the fashion is fleeting and is, indeed, as good as obsolete; and the next boom was of Tagore, the least energeticomaniac of them all. I conclude, once more, that the age is really characterless: like Mr. Wells, it is versatile and nothing more. It will be recorded in history as doing everything badly.

Not to leave the subject without a bone for the dog, I may say that my own view is that our immediate future is along the route which, beginning with brilliant common sense, conducts to beauty by way of wisdom. We are all sensible at bottom; and good sense is our proper starting-place. Hence, when, as now, we find ourselves floundering, we ought to return to our base in common sense and resume from there. Common sense mellowed and experienced is wisdom; and wisdom in its ripeness is beauty. Young men, I say, first learn to write common sense; then study to be wise, and beauty will afterwards be added to you.

NEW STANDARDS IN ART
AND LITERATURE

The secret of practical success is to have defined and possible aims, and to adapt one's means toward them. Vague aims and, still more, unattainable aims are destructive of common sense in practical affairs. Everything in this sphere depends upon the calculable and the calculated; upon cutting one's coat according to one's cloth; upon precisely adapting means to a precise end; upon the correct use of tools for a given piece of work.

But what distinguishes art from practical conduct is the substitution, as end, of the impossible and unattainable for the possible and attainable. Art cannot have a circumscribed and limited aim, on peril of reducing its votaries to the rank of craftsmen simply. Craft has its aim as good craftsmanship, the production of the intended effect by the most economical use of means. But art, though it employs craftsmanship, has not the aim of good workmanship, or the production of an intended effect. Its aim is the unattainable, the unrealizable, the impossible; and all real works of art are the by-products of a striving toward what can never be produced. Only in this aspect is art comparable with religion, whose works likewise are by-products, addenda to the search for the unrealizable Kingdom of Heaven. An art without unattainable aims is at best journeyman art, never master art; and at worst it substitutes refinement of technique for culture of the spirit.

In no respect is modern art more defective than in precisely this, and because of precisely this: that its standards and aims have ceased to be impossible. We are all practical men nowadays, and the doctrines of business have become the working rules of professed artists and writers. Just such and such a work must be produced; and just such and such a preparation, assemblage of materials, and even personal experience, are necessary toward it—just so much and no more to produce the intended effect. Is it to present a section of American life or a cameo of life in Patagonia? One must have seen so much of the original, have been there for a sufficient length of time, to entitle one to the defined impression; and with this material the defined aim of presentation is presumably accomplished.

Critics, of course, succumb to this deadening influence more easily than artists. After all, artists have a conscience sensitive to the degree to which they are artists; and no amount of skill in craftsmanship, finesse, and technique, or the approval these receive, really stills an artistic conscience that has once waked and cried in the night. That artists are still capable of a degree of shame in presence even of their most successful works is evidence that the spirit of religion or the pursuit of the unattainable is not yet dead in them. Critics, as a rule, have no such conscience: they are theologians—not saints. What are by-products for the artists are end-products for the critic; and since the critic is naturally unaware of the unattainable aim entertained by the artist, he can, even if he be so minded, divine its character and intensity only from the by-product it induces, for the invisible tree of art is known only to the artist, and the critic can judge only by the visible fruit.

For this reason it is exceedingly difficult to reinfuse art with its necessary impossible aims when once they cease to exist in the minds of artists. They are like a virtue of which the original possessor has lost the secret. The critic can see clearly enough that something has gone out of art: the fruit that drops from the invisible tree is not what it used to be; it is no longer paradisaical. At the same time the cause remains unknown and indiscoverable; and, in any case, much more than an analysis of the taste and flavour of the fruit is necessary to renew the life of the tree. Restoring art that has lost its unattainable aim is like attempting by reason to restore the youth of a religion. The source can be affected only by a fresh source, not by any of its own issues; and, in fact, no religion that has once died has experienced resurrection, and no art that has once declined has ever been renewed from within. Art cannot save art; and still less, when artists have failed art, can critics save it.

Hitherto there have been many happy accidents in the history of art in the West. Art has descended Parnassus through several millennia by a series of reinforced impulses, each phase at some critical moment of its development receiving from a superior stream a new force and direction. The Greek stream, at the moment when it was about to die of its own impulse, received by accident a tributary of Egyptian art which raised its source considerably above its original level, for the Greeks, in the absence of Egyptian tradition, and even with it, were 'children'. Still later the art of the early Middle Ages was miraculously saved from imminent death by renaissant contact with the classical sources, which themselves had been reinforced from the Egyptian. Later still, and on a different plane, what has been the history of European art since the Renaissance, but the finding of a common level? Here Spain had something to give France; here Holland something to give England;

and recently Russia something to give the Teutonic world. But these are trivialities only, details of local distribution. Cultures much on à level cannot profoundly affect each other; not renaissances, but only 'movements', spring from the congress of coeval cultures. And ever since the Renaissance all European art has been nothing more than waves affecting waves. There has been no new tidal movement.

The more conscientious—or, rather, conscious—of both artists and critics are aware of the facts even though they are ignorant of the cause. Everywhere the rumour runs that art is dead: not too loud a rumour, lest the world lose hope; but sufficiently loud to be plainly heard, and uttered with more anxiety than is compatible with doubt of its veracity. But before the fact shall be publicly known and admitted that 'the King is dead', shall we not try first to revive him, and, if that fail, to prepare his successor? Necromancy has its place here maybe; and in the absence of necromancy perhaps a pseudo-idol may be manufactured: a visible and imposing dummy for an invisible king.

It is in this light that the recent attempts to infuse into art the blood of savage cultures may be understood: as also the various and numerous schools of art-invention. What profounder sources are accessible than our common aboriginal racial roots, the black, the red, the yellow? Let us look to West Africa, to Tahiti, to the Mayas and Aztecs, to China and Japan; concurrently let invention be tried: imagism, cubism, Joyceism, planes, solids, angles, and every verbal and geometric device. Alas, our aboriginal roots are just not dynamic sources. The invisible tree of art, like the tree Yggdrasill, is fed from the sky downward: its roots are in Heaven, in the impossible, in the never as yet, and perhaps never to be, actualized; not in history but in imagination, not in any past, however ancient, but in a future only potential. Invention likewise has its limitations in the already given; and combination is not creation. Neither by transfusion of blood from inferior races nor by any fresh combination of known elements can art be restored to life. Neither black magic nor sleight of hand can raise our dead.

But is the case hopeless, and is culture irrevocably doomed? There is a remedy and not an impossible one: its name is ancient India. Ancient India stands in the same relation to us 'children' of Europe as ancient Egypt occupied toward the 'children' of Greece. Europe to-day is ancient Greece writ large. India, moreover, is our most ancient parent; our oldest racial ancestor; our Adam and Eve. Truly enough, her visage is wrinkled with age, and her words are a mumble of incoherence. But so must, no doubt, have appeared to the Greek child the ancient wisdom of Egypt. Pythagoras is not reported to have found it easy to persuade Greece to go to school to Egypt. On the other hand, we are not obliged to speculate darkly in the philosophy of India. The philosophies of India are without exception no more than mummies, the enshrined corpses of once living ideas, and dead very long since. And, even if they could be revived, art can no more be saved by philosophy than by art itself. The dead cannot raise the dead. Nor need we spend any time with the Indian antiquarians. Scholarship of whatever degree is barren. No—we have, by grace, accessible to us in the remains of ancient India, something infinitely more living than philosophies, and infinitely more inspiring than scholarship. We have a literature translatable and translated into our own tongue, of such dimensions and qualities that its chief work alone, the *Mahabharata,* towers over all subsequent literature as the Pyramids look over the Memphian sands.

II

TALKS WITH
KATHERINE MANSFIELD

II

TALKS WITH
KATHERINE MANSFIELD

Everybody knows that Katherine Mansfield spent her last days in the Gurdjieff Institute at Fontainebleau, and the letters and diaries which Mr. Middleton Murry has now published bear ample testimony to the value she attached both to the institute and to the system of training employed there. Many questions have been asked concerning the particular advantage other than health which Katherine Mansfield hoped to derive from it all. Had she come to the end of her writing impulse? But she was still full of sketches and plans for future stories, and even a novel or two. Was she dissatisfied with her craftsmanship, and did she hope to improve it under a special method of training? But she was always dissatisfied and always improving herself. From the age of about twenty-one, when she showed me her first sketch, and I published it in the *New Age*, to her death at thirty-three, at a moment when she was planning to write again after some months' rest, she worked, as few writers work, to develop and perfect her style in the agony of conviction that so far it was only embryonic.

Some months before she went into the institute at Fontainebleau she told me that she could not read any of the stories she had written without feeling self-contempt. 'There is not one', she said, 'that I dare show to God.' It therefore did not need the institute to intensify her wish to excel in her craftsmanship; and, indeed, the institute was not a school of literary art, nor was she under any illusion that writing could be taught there. The real reason, and the only reason, that led Katherine Mansfield to the Gurdjieff Institute was less dissatisfaction with her craftsmanship than dissatisfaction with herself; less dissatisfaction with her stories than with the attitude toward life implied in them; less dissatisfaction with her own and contemporary literature than with literature.

I had many conversations with her on this topic during the years of our acquaintance, and particularly during the months preceding her death. She was even more explicit on these occasions than in her letters and diaries. 'Suppose', she used to say, 'that I could succeed in writing as well as Shakespeare. It would be lovely, but what then? There is something wanting in literary art even at its highest. Literature is not enough.'

'The greatest literature', she said, 'is still only mere literature if it has not a purpose commensurate with its art. Presence or absence of purpose distinguishes literature from mere literature, and the elevation of the purpose distinguishes literature within literature. That is merely literary that has no other object than to please. Minor literature has a didactic object. But the greatest literature of all—the literature that scarcely exists—has not merely an æsthetic object, nor merely a didactic object, but, in addition, a creative object: that of subjecting its readers to a real and at the same time illuminating experience. Major literature, in short, is an initiation into truth.'

'But where do we stand in relation to that?' I asked. 'Where is the writer with the keys of initiation upon him?'

This was Katherine Mansfield's introduction to the Gurdjieff Institute, and the object of her travel there. For she realized that it is not writing as writing that needs criticism, correction, and perfection, so much as the mind, character, and personality of the writer. One must become more to write better. Certainly this does not exclude the possibility of great improvement in technique without the aid of any system of personal training. On the other hand, when, as in Katherine Mansfield's case, the improvement of one's technique by the ordinary means has ceased to be possible, or has fallen under the law of diminishing returns (yielding too small a result for the effort expended), then the adoption of an entirely new means, such as special self-training, becomes imperative if the will to perfection is still as active as it was in her.

I saw Katherine Mansfield almost every day in the institute, and we had many long talks together. For months she was quite content not to be writing or even reading. We had a common surprise in contrasting our current attitude towards literature with the craze we had both experienced for many years. What has come over us? she would ask whimsically. Are we dead? Or was our love of literature an affectation, which had now dropped off like a mask? Every now and then, on the other hand, a return of the old enthusiasm would be experienced. She would begin a story and confide to me that she was rather enjoying the thrill of writing again. The following day she had torn it up, quite cheerfully, and with a grimace of humour. Premature delivery! She was under contract, I believe, to write a number of stories for one publisher or another, and many times she spoke of it as an obligation. But greater even than her wish to keep her engagement with her publishers was her resolution not to write stories in the old style. Her new stories were to be different. How different only she had any real conception; and, moreover, she kept it to herself, not even confiding it to her diaries or her most intimate letters. It was, in fact, a conception to be brooded upon, and not written about— a conception that slowly arose within a new state of being and understanding; a conception, therefore, inexpressible in words until its inner metamorphoses had been completed. I read her diaries in vain for a real trace of the new idea that had begun to dawn in Katherine Mansfield. She writes in them repeatedly of new stories, but never of the new attitude to be implied and manifested in them. She would write, as before, with all her old qualities vivified and illuminated; she would continue to employ her marvellously microscopic observation of men and women. But her attitude was to have undergone a change. In a word, she would have a new purpose in writing—a purpose not only to gratify and instruct, but to initiate and create.

One day, shortly before her death, she sent for me to come to her room; she had something very important to tell me. When I arrived, she was in high spirits. Her face shone as if she had been on Sinai.

'What is it, Katherine?' I asked. 'What makes you so happy?'

'I have found my idea', she said. 'I've got it at last. It arose, of course, out of a personal experience. Katya has felt something that she never felt in her life before, and Katya understands something she never understood before.'

I cannot recall the exact words in which she proceeded to expound her new idea, or, rather, new attitude toward life and literature. It was, moreover, adumbrated with the aid of silences during which I thought as intensely as she on the subject; and from these she would emerge with a fresh suggestion or an improved formulation of a previous opinion. I can only record fragments, and the final impression in her mind. Briefly, the conclusion was this: to make the commonplace virtues as attractive as ordinarily the vices are made: to present the good as the witty, the adventurous, the romantic, the gay, the alluring; and the evil as the platitudinous, the dull, the conventional, the solemn, and the unattractive.

'I have not been able to think', she said, 'that I should not have made such observations as I *have* made of people, however cruel they may seem. After all, I *did* observe those things, and I had to set them down. I've been a camera. But that's just the point. I've been a selective camera, and it has been my attitude that has determined the selection; with the result that my slices of life (thank you, Mr. Phillpotts!) have been partial, misleading, and a little malicious. Further, they have had no other purpose than to record my attitude, which in itself stood in need of change if it was to become active instead of passive. Altogether, I've been not only a mere camera, but I've been a selective camera, and a selective camera without a creative principle. And, like everything unconscious, the result has been evil.'

'Well, and what is your new plan?'

'To widen first the scope of my camera, and then to employ it for a conscious purpose—that of representing life not merely as it appears to a certain attitude, but as it appears to another and different attitude, a creative attitude.'

'What do you mean by a creative attitude?' I asked.

'You must help me out, Orage,' she replied, 'if I miss the words. But I mean something like this. Life can be made to appear anything by presenting only one aspect of it; and every attitude in us—every mood, I mean to say—sees only one aspect. Assuming that this attitude is more or less permanent in any given writer, and insusceptible of being changed by his own will, he is bound to present only the correspondent aspect of life, and, at the same time, to do no more than present it. He is passively victimised by the partial vision imposed on him, and this, in its turn, is without dynamic quality. Such reflections of life have the effect of reflections in a looking-glass of real objects; that is, none whatever.'

'Your idea is, then, to affect life and no longer just to reflect it?'

K

'Oh, that is too big,' she said. 'You must not laugh at me. Help me to express myself.'

She continued with occasional suggestions of words, and finally completed the sketch of her new attitude.

'There are in life as many aspects as attitudes toward it; and aspects change with attitudes. At present we see life, generally speaking, in only a passive aspect because we bring only a passive attitude to bear upon it. Could we change our attitude, we should not only see life differently, but life itself would come to *be* different. Life would undergo a change of appearance because we ourselves had undergone a change in attitude. I'm aware, for example, of a recent change of attitude in myself: and at once not only my old stories have come to look different to me, but life itself looks different. I could not write my old stories again, or any more like them: and not because I do not see the same detail as before, but because somehow or other the pattern is different. The old details now make another pattern; and this perception of a new pattern is what I call a creative attitude toward life.'

'You mean,' I said, 'that while the details of life—the forms, colours, sounds, etc.—remain the same, the pattern under which you arrange them is now different, owing to your change of attitude? Formerly, for example, being yourself in a mood, say, of resentment, you have selected and presented your observations of life in a pattern of, say, a cross of amused suffering? Your present attitude, being creative, and not, like resentment, simply reactive, arranges the same details, but in a different pattern; in a pattern to present, say, the descent from the cross?'

'I wish I dare mean half as much as that', Katherine Mansfield said, 'but really my idea is much smaller. Perhaps not, though, if I come to think about it. Do you think it is very presumptuous of me?'

I reassured her, and she continued:

'An artist communicates not his vision of the world, but the attitude that results in his vision; not his dream, but his dream-state; and as his attitude is passive, negative, or indifferent, so he reinforces in his readers the corresponding state of mind. Now, most writers are merely passive; in fact, they aim only at representing life, as they say, with the consequence that their readers for the most part become even more passive, even more spectatorial, and we have a world of Peeping Toms with fewer and fewer Lady Godivas to ride by. What I am trying to say is that a new attitude to life on the part of writers would first see life different and then make it different.'

'Have you come to any practical conclusion as regards the writing of stories?' I asked. 'Do you see the possibility of a new kind of story? How will your new idea work out in practice?'

Katherine Mansfield showed me some fragments of beginnings of stories, all of which she tore up.

'I have begun many times,' she said, 'but I am not yet ready, it seems. However, the idea is clear enough, and I shall carry it out one day. Here is an example. I won't say it is one I shall ever write, but it will serve as an illustration. Two people fall in love and marry. One, or perhaps both of them, have had previous affairs, the remains of which still linger like ghosts in the new home. Both wish to forget, but the ghosts still walk. How can this situation be presented? Ordinarily a writer, such as the late lamented Katherine Mansfield, would bring her passive, selective, and resentful attitude to bear upon it, and the result would be one of her famous satiric sketches reinforcing in her readers the attitude in herself. Or, peradventure, some didacticist would treat of the situation, and present us with a homily on the importance of sacrifice. Others would treat it pathetically or solemnly or psychologically or melodramatically or humorously, each according to his own passive attitude or normal mood.

'But I should represent it as my present attitude sees it, as a common adventure in ghost laying. Thanks to some change in me since I have been here, I see any such situation as an opportunity for the exercise and employment of all the intelligence, invention, imagination, bravery, endurance, and, in fact, all the virtues of the most attractive hero and heroine. Think of the subtlety necessary on both sides to maintain a mutual state of love which both naturally and sincerely wish to maintain, as, of course, everybody does. Think of how they would try to lay the ghosts in each other and in themselves. Suppose them to be jointly competing for the divine laurel and living and loving as an art. I can see such a scope for subtlety of observation that Henry James might appear myopic. At the same time, no quality need necessarily remain unemployed; but every power of the artist might be brought into play.'

'You would not necessarily have a happy ending?' I asked.

'Not by any means. The problem might prove to be too big. Heroes and heroines are not measured either by what they passively endure or by what they actually achieve, but by the quantity and quality of the effort they put forth. The reader's sympathy would be maintained by the continuity and variety of the effort of one or both of the characters, by their indomitable renewal of the struggle with ever fresh invention. Usually our "heroes" flag in their resources; they sulk after their first failure, or simply repeat the tactics which have already failed. And we are asked to admire their endurance or sympathise with their suffering or laugh at their ineptitude. I wish the laugh to be with the heroes. Let them anticipate the passive spectator and act as if the problem were theirs only to solve. That, roughly, is my new idea.'

'And you really see your way to writing stories with it?'

'I see the way, but I still have to go it.'

Only a few weeks later Katherine Mansfield was dead. I saw her a few hours before her death, and she was still radiant in her new attitude.

III

READERS AND WRITERS

III

READERS AND WRITERS

THE FASHION OF ANTI-PURITANISM

The anti-Puritanism of the professed anti-Puritans is very little, if any, better than the Puritanism they oppose. The two parties divide the honours of our dislike fairly evenly between them. Puritanism is a fanatical devotion to a single aspect of virtue—namely, to morality. It assumes that Life is moral and nothing else; that Power, Wisdom, Truth, Beauty, and Love are all of no account in comparison with Goodness; and doing so it offends our judgement of the nature of Virtue, which is that Virtue is wholeness or a balance of all the aspects of God. Anti-Puritanism, on the other hand, denies all the affirmations of Puritanism, but without affirming anything on its own account. It denies that Life is exclusively moral, but it does not affirm that life is anything else; it destroys the false absolute of Puritanism, but it is silent to the extent of tacitly denying that there is any absolute whatsoever. This being the case, our choice between Puritanism and anti-Puritanism is between a false absolute and no absolute, between a one-sided truth and no truth at all. We are bound to be half-hearted upon either side, since the thing itself is only half a thing.

I am not likely to revise my opinions about virtue from the School of Marx and his disciple Kautsky. Marx was another flamen, a priest, that is to say, of one aspect only of reality—in this case the economic. That the moral cant of a particular age tends to represent the economic interest of the dominant class is, of course, a truism; but there is a world of difference between moral cant and morality—and the latter is as uniform throughout all history as the former is variable. Moreover, it is not by any means always the case that the interests of the dominant class of capitalism are identical with Puritanism. The interests of capitalism to-day are decidedly with anti-Puritanism, in so far as the effects of anti-Puritanism are to break up family life, to restrict births and to cultivate eugenics. What could suit capitalism better than to atomise the last surviving natural grouping of individuals and to breed for the servile State? The anti-Puritan propagandas of Malthusianism and eugenics are not carried on, either, by Marxians, but by the wealthy classes. Because he is a shopkeeper, the Anglo-Saxon is to-day an anti-Puritan in these matters.

POPULAR PHILOSOPHY

The difficulty of popular philosophical discussion is not insuperable. It is all a matter of style. Mr. Bertrand Russell, for example, manages by means of an excellent style to make philosophy as easy to understand, and as entrancing to follow, as certain writers have made the equally difficult subject of economics. It is, in fact, the business of professional thinkers to popularise their subject and to procure for their Muse as many devotees as possible. In the case of Mr. Bertrand Russell, his admirable style has been put into the service of the most abominable philosophy ever formulated. He is an accidentalist of the most thoroughgoing kind who denies that life has any meaning or purpose. Life appeared, he says, by chance, and will disappear, probably for good, with the cooling of the sun; and he sings like a doomed

cricket on a dissolving iceberg. But it is all the more
strange in my judgement that a man who thinks thus can
write as Mr. Russell writes. There is a contradiction somewhere between the simple richness of his style and the
Spartan poverty of his ideas. He thinks glacially, but his
style is warm. I suspect that if he were psycho-analysed,
Mr. Bertrand Russell would turn out to be a walking
contradiction. In a word, I don't believe he believes a word
he says! That tone, that style, them there gestures—they
betray the stage-player of the spirit.

A philosophy written in a popular style is not, of course,
the same thing as a popular philosophy. 'From a popular
philosophy and a philosophical populace, good sense deliver
us', said Coleridge, meaning to say that a philosophy whose
substance, and not whose expression only, has been adapted
to the populace, is in all probability false, and is certainly
superficial. For in his *Lay Sermons,* published a hundred
years ago, Coleridge supplemented the foregoing remark
by deploring the 'long and ominous eclipse of philosophy,
the usurpation of that venerable name by physical and
psychological empiricism, and the non-existence of a learned
and philosophical *public.*' Between a philosophic public and
a philosophic populace there is the same distinction as
between the 'public' that reads, let us say, Sedlak, and the
'populace' that reads, let us say, Mr. H. G. Wells. Mr. Wells
is a popular philosopher; but that is manifestly not the same
thing as a writer who is trying to make philosophy popular.

THE END OF FICTION

Fiction nowadays, we are told, is not what it used to be.
We are told that it is the modern university. It is certainly
a very obliging medium. But on this very account it is as
delusive as it is obliging. It receives impressions easily,

readily adapts itself to every kind of material, and assumes at the word of command any and every mood. But precisely because it does these things, the effects it produces are transient. Lightly come, lightly go; and if, as has been said, fiction is the modern reader's university, it is a school in which he learns everything and forgets everything. Modern as I am, and hopeful as I am of modernity, I cannot think that the predominance of fiction, even of such fiction as is written to-day, is a good sign; and when we see that it leads nowhere, that the people who read much of it never read anything else, and that it is an intellectual cul-de-sac, our alarm at the phenomenon is the greater. What kind of minds do we expect to develop on a diet of forty parts fiction to two of all other forms of literature? Assuming the free libraries to be the continuation schools of the public, what is their value if the only lessons taken in them are the lessons of fiction? I will not dwell on the obvious discouragement the figures are to every serious *writer*, for the effect on the readers must be worse.

THE CRITERIA OF CULTURE

The suppression of the display of feeling, or, better, the control of the display of feeling, is the first condition of thought, and only those who have aimed at writing with studied simplicity, studied lucidity, and studied detachment realize the amount of feeling that has to be trained to run quietly in harness. The modern failure (as compared with the success of the Greeks) to recognize feeling as an essential element of lucidity and the rest of the virtues of literary form is due to an excess of fiction. Just because fiction expresses everything it really impresses nothing. Its feeling evaporates as fast as it exudes. The sensation, nevertheless, is pleasant, for the reader appears to be witnessing genuine feeling genuinely expressing itself; and he fails to remember that what is true of a person is likely to be true of a book, that the more apparent, obvious, and demonstrated the feelings, the more superficial, unreal, and transient they probably are. As a matter of cold-blooded fact, it has been clearly shown during the course of the war that precisely our most 'passionate' novelists have been our least patriotic citizens. I name no names, since they are known to everybody.

Culture I define as being, amongst other things, a capacity for subtle discrimination of words and ideas. Epictetus made the discrimination of words the foundation of moral training, and it is true enough that every stage of moral progress is indicated by the degree of our perception of the meaning of words. Tell me what words have a particular interest for you, and I will tell you what class of the world-school you are in. Tell me what certain words mean for you and I will tell you what you mean for the world of thought. One of the most subtle words, and one of the key-words of culture, is Simplicity. Can you discriminate between natural simplicity and studied simplicity, between Nature and Art? In appearance they are indistinguishable, but in reality they are æons apart; and whoever has learned to distinguish between them is entitled to regard himself as on the way to culture. Originality is another keyword, and its subtlety may be suggested by a paradox which was a commonplace among the Greeks; namely, that the most original minds strive to conceal their originality, and that the master-minds succeed. Contrast this counsel of perfect originality with the counsels given in our own day, in which the aim of originality is directed to appearing original—you will be brought thereby face to face with still another key-idea of Culture, the relation of Appearance to Reality. All these exercises in Culture are elementary, however, in comparison with the master-problem of 'disinterestedness'. No word in the English language is more difficult to define or better worth attempting to define. Somewhere or other in its capacious folds it contains all the ideas of ethics, and even, I should say, of religion. The *Bhagavad Gita* (to name only one classic) can be summed up in the word. Duty is only a pale equivalent of it. I venture to say that whoever has understood the meaning of 'disinterestedness' is not far off understanding the goal of human culture.

CONVALESCENCE AFTER NEWSPAPER

Matthew Arnold used to say that to get his feet wet spoiled his style for days. But there is a far worse enemy of style than natural damp: it is too much newspaper-reading. Too much newspaper not only spoils one's style, it takes off the edge of one's taste, so that I know not what grindstones are necessary to put it on again. Indulgent readers, I have been compelled for some weeks to read too much newspaper, with the consequence that at the end of my task I was not only certain that my little of style was gone, but I was indifferent in my taste. The explanation of the *reductio ad absurdum* to which an overdose of newspaper leads is to be found, I think, in the uniformity, mass and collectivity of newspaper literature. The writing that fills the Press is neither individual nor does it aim at individuality. If a citizens' meeting, a jury, or the House of Commons were to perform the feat of making its voice heard, the style of their oracles would be perfect newspaper. But literature, I need not say, is not made after this fashion; nor is it inspired by such performances. Literature, like all art, is, above everything, individual expression. *Gardez-vous!* I do not mean that literature is a personal expression of the personal opinion of the writer. On the contrary, it is the role of newspaper to give common expression to personal opinions, but it is the function of literature to give personal expression

to common opinions. And since it is only personal expression
that provokes and inspires personal expression, from newspapers one can derive no stimulus to literature, but only the
opposite, a disrelish and a distate.

How to recover one's health after newspaper poisoning
is a problem. To plunge back forthwith into books was, for
me, an impossibility. It was necessary to begin again from
the very beginning and gradually to accustom myself to the
taste for literature again. Rearranging my books, and throwing away the certainly-done-with was, I found, as useful a
preliminary tonic as any other I could devise. In particular
there is a satisfaction in throwing out books which makes
this medicine as pleasant as it is tonic. It visibly reduces the
amount left to be read; there is then not so much on one's
plate that the appetite revolts at the prospect. And who can
throw away a book without glancing into it to make sure
that it will never again be wanted? Picking and tasting in
this indeliberate way, the invalid appetite is half coaxed to
sit up and take proper nourishment. This destruction and
reconstruction I certainly found recovering, and I can therefore commend them to be included in the pharmacopœias.

Another nourishing exercise when you are in this state is
the overhauling of your accumulations of memoranda,
cuttings and notebooks. I have sat for hours during the last
few days, like a beaver unbuilding its dam, turning out,
with a view to destroying their contents, drawer after
drawer and shelf upon shelf. It is fatal to set about the
operation with any tenderness. Your aim must be to destroy
everything which does not command you to spare it. The
tragic recklessness of the procedure is the virtue of the
medicine. As a matter of fact there is little or nothing now
left in my drawers for future use. Nearly all my paper-boats
have been burned, including some three-decked galleons
which were originally designed to bring me fame. No
matter; the Rubicon is crossed, and to be on the other side

of newspaper with no more than a thin portfolio of notes is to have escaped cheaply.

For the humour if it, however, I will record a careful exception. It appears, after all, that I was not so mad as I seemed. Perchance newspaper, being only a feigned literature, induces only a feigned madness. Be it as it may. I find that my current notebook, though as handy and tempting to be destroyed as any other, was nevertheless destroyed only after the cream of it had been whipped into the permanent book which I have kept through many rages for a good many years. The extracts are here before me as I write in convalescence. It is amusing to me to observe, moreover, that their cream is not very rich. Much better has gone into the bonfire. Why, then, did I save these and sacrifice those? Look at a few of them. 'Nobody's anything always'—is there aught irrecoverable in that to have compelled me to spare it? 'Lots of window, but no warehouse'—a remark, I fancy, intended to hit somebody or other very hard indeed —but *does* it? Is any of the present company fitted with a cap? 'The judgement of the world is good, but few can put it into words.' That is a premonitory symptom, you will observe, of a remark made a few lines above to the effect that literature is a personal expression of a common opinion or judgement. I have plainly remembered it. Apropos of the *New Age,* I must have told somebody, and stolen home to write it down, that its career is that of a rocking-horse, all ups and downs but never any getting forward. It is too true to be wholly amusing; let me horse-laugh at it and pass it on. 'A simple style is like sleep, it will not come by effort.' Not altogether true, but true enough. The rest are not much worse or better, and the puzzle is to explain why those should be taken and these left.

Again apropos, may a physician who has healed himself offer this piece of advice? Read your own notebooks often. I have known some people who have a library of notebooks worth a dukedom, who never once looked into them after having filled them. That is collecting mania pure and simple. From another offensive angle, what a confession of inferior taste is made in preferring the notebooks of others to one's own. A little more self-respect in this matter is clearly necessary if your conversation is to be personal at all; for in all probability the references and quotations you make *without* the authority of your own collection are hackneyed. They are the reach-me-downs of every encyclopædia. Is this the reason that the vast majority of current quotations are as worn as they are; that a constant reader, forewarned of the subject about to be dealt with, is usually forearmed against the tags he will find employed in it? In any case, the advice I have just given is the corrective of this depressing phenomenon of modern writing. You have only to trade in your own notebooks to be, and to give the air of being, truly original.

Browsing is a rather more advanced regimen for convalescence than the rearrangement of books. The latter can be performed without the smallest taste for reading. It is a matter of sizing them up, and any bookseller's apprentice can do it. But browsing means dipping into the contents here and there; it is both a symptom of returning health and a means to it. In the last few days I must have nibbled in a hundred different pastures, chiefly, I think, in the pastures of books about books. De Quincey, Matthew Arnold, Bagehot, Macaulay, Johnson, etc.—what meadows, what lush grass, what feed! After all, one begins to say, literature cannot be unsatisfying that fed such bulls and that so plumped their minds. It cannot be only a variety of newspaper. Thus a new link with health is established, and one becomes able to take one's books again. Here I should end, but that a last observation in the form of a question occurs to me. Is not, or can not, a taste for literature be acquired by the same means by which it can be re-acquired? Are not the child and the invalid similar? In that case the foregoing directions may be not altogether useless.

THE DECLINE OF FREE INTELLIGENCE

Pure intelligence I should define as displaying itself in disinterested interest in things; in things, that is to say, of no *personal* advantage, but only of general, public, or universal importance. Interest (to turn the cat in the pan) is the growing end of the mind, and its direction and strength are marked by a motiveless curiosity to know; it reveals itself, while it is still active, as a love of knowledge for its own sake. Later on it often appears that this motiveless love had a motive; in other words, the knowledge acquired under its impulse is discovered in the end to 'come in handy', and to have been of use. But the process of acquiring this knowledge is for the most part indeliberate, unaware of any other aim than that of the satisfaction of curiosity; utility is remote from its mind. This is what I have called disinterested interest, and it is this free intelligence of which it appears to me that there is a diminishing amount in our day. Were it not the case, the fortunes of the really free Press would be much brighter than they are. An organ of free opinion would not need to discover a utilitarian attraction for its free opinions, but would be able to command a sale on its own merits. Such, indeed, is the case in several European countries, notably in France, Italy, and Germany. I am told that it is the case also in Bohemia (in which country there is not only no illiterate, but no unread adult) and in the provinces of Yugo-Slavia. In these countries a journal of opinions can live without providing its readers with any commercial or specialist bribe in the way of exclusive utilitarian information: it can live, that is to say, by the sale of its free intelligence. Happy countries—in one sense of the word; happy if also tragical; for their existence is not always, at any rate, a paradise for the rich, a hell for the poor, and a purgatory for the able!

To what is due this decline amongst us of free intelligence? There are several explanations possible, though none is wholly satisfying. It can be attributed to the industrialization of our own country, a metamorphosis of occupation which has been longer in being in England than anywhere else. The economic balance between primary and secondary production has been for a longer period lost in this country than elsewhere, with the consequence that we have been the first to exhibit the effects of over-industrialization in the loss of the free intelligence associated with primary production. The other nations may be expected to follow suit as the same metamorphosis overtakes them. Another explanation is the reaction against the intellectualism of the nineteenth century. It is a familiar topic, but it is obvious that if faith in the ultimate *use* of intelligence is lost, men become cynical in regard to the passion itself. Let us suppose that every love affair always and invariably ended in disappointment or disaster. Let us suppose that it became the accepted belief that such would always be the case. Would it not soon become fashionable to nip the first stirrings of love in the bud, and to salt its path whenever its shoots began to appear? The nineteenth century reached its climax in a vast disappointment with science, with the intellect, with intellectualism. The fifth act of the thrilling drama inaugurated after the French Revolution closed in utter weariness and ennui. It was no wonder that the twentieth century opened in a return to impulse and in a corresponding reaction from intellectuality. That the reaction has gone too far is the very disease we are now trying to diagnose; for only an excessive reaction towards impulse and away from thought can account for the poverty of free intelligence. Sooner or later, the pendulum must be set free again, if not in this country,

L

then in America, or in some of the countries whose rebirth we are now witnessing. It cannot be the will of God that free intelligence should be extinguished from the planet; the world, somehow or other, must be made safe for intelligence as well as for democracy.

My last guess at the origin of the phenomenon is the decline of the religious spirit. Religion, I conceive, is the study and practice of perfection, and it is summed up in the text: 'Be ye perfect, even as your Father in Heaven is perfect'. This impossible and infinite aim includes, as a matter of course, the employment and development of intelligence as one of the most powerful aids to perfection. Fools, the Indian Scriptures inform us, can enter heaven, but only wise men know how to stay there. And if the perfection we seek is to be lasting and incorruptible, it is certain that an infinite amount of intelligence will be necessary to its accomplishment. The loss of the belief in the perfectibility of the human spirit, in the religious duty of perfection, might easily account for the diminution of our regard for one of the chief instruments of perfection, namely, intelligence. Why should we strive to set the crooked straight, since it is not only impossible, but is no duty of ours? And why labour with the instrumental means when the end is of no value? None of these explanations, however, really satisfies me.

The free Press is more severely criticized by its readers than the 'kept' Press by its clientele. The reason is, no doubt, that in comparison with the 'kept' Press it protests its freedom and sets itself up on a pedestal. Every 'excuse' is consequently denied to it, and the smallest complaint is enlarged to a grievance. The 'kept' Press may be caught in flagrant self-contradiction, in lies, in chicanery of all kinds, in every form of intellectual and other dishonesty—it continues to be read and 'followed' as if the oracle were infallible. No newspaper in this country has ever died of exposure; many live by being found out. The free Press, on the other hand, has often for its readers not only the most exigent of critics, but the most contradictory. They are not only hard to please (which is a merit), but their reasons for being pleased, or the reverse, are bewilderingly various. And, moreover, when they are pleased they are usually silent, and when they are displeased they cease to buy the journal.

IV

ART

IV

ART

We may agree with Croce that all art is expression without agreeing with him that all expression is art. *Qua* expression, expression is—expression; and a quite different concept must enter before we can convert the equation into 'expression is art'. Nor is the matter settled by attempting to discover which expressions are art and which are not, since the 'art' of the expression is not so much in the expression as in the effect produced. Putting it another way, we can say, however, that those expressions, and only those, are 'artistic' that produce the effect of art by deliberate designs. But what is this 'effect of art'? It is sometimes imagined that an artistic effect is one that is 'felt'; in other words, it is said to be an emotion of some kind. In this case, the success of a 'work of art' is assumed to lie in the transfer of the emotion of the artist to the experience of the beholder; and the latter is said to 'appreciate' the work because he has been made to reproduce the emotions of the artist who created it. Or, again, it is sometimes assumed that a work of art is successful in proportion to the number and quality of the 'ideas' it stimulates in the spectator or hearer or reader. A given quantity of ideas or a given quality of ideas, when it reaches a certain degree of intensity, is said to be the result of art and to entitle the canvas or sonata or essay to be regarded as a work of art. Here, too, the success is assumed to be due to the transfer of the artist's ideas to his beholder, hearer or

reader. Considerable difficulties arise from accepting either
of these theories or any combination or modification of
them. For instance, it is well known that artists sometimes
'convey' much more emotion and many more ideas than
they themselves have ever experienced. This is particularly
true of musicians and painters. Again, the theory assumes
that the artist is in a high degree of emotion when expressing
himself, or that he is, as we say, 'full of ideas'—states of mind
which, however desirable in themselves, are certainly not
conducive to the production of a work of art. As regards
the beholder, the same difficulties arise. Must he call a work
of art the piece that has 'moved' him; or the piece that has
stirred the greatest number of ideas in him? But in that case,
very low forms of art and, often, no art at all, must be given
the credit; for we have all felt considerable emotion and
experienced many ideas from subjects which by common
consent are not in the category of art at all. The conclusion
to be drawn is the somewhat startling one, that art has
nothing to do either with emotions or with ideas. Neither
feeling nor intellect, in the precise sense, is engaged either
in the production or in the appreciation of a work of art;
but some power of the mind to which it is difficult to give
an exact name. Let us suppose, however, that, in the main,
emotions derive from the subconscious, and 'ideas' from the
conscious. Art, having to do with neither, can then be
assumed to be the medium for the expression of the superconscious, the characteristic activity of which we may call
contemplation. With this classification, the nature and
purpose of art become not only intelligible, but simple. Art
arises from the creative contemplation of the artist and
arouses in the beholders a corresponding appreciative contemplation. Both artist and critic are on the superconscious
plane: the one creating symbols for its expression and the
other experiencing its life in contemplation. All art thus
plunges the beholder into a high state of reverie or wonder

or contemplation or meditation; and that is both its nature and its purpose. We should suspect a work professing to be art when it arouses either caution or thought. Unless it can still both of these inferior states, and arouse us to contemplation, it is human, all too human.

V

WHAT IS THE SOUL?

V

WHAT IS THE SOUL?

The *New Age* has lately been gently chided for using the words 'God' and the 'soul' as if they conveyed a definite meaning.

Yes, and if I could have been convinced of our error, I should have been by the argument.

Why, what was it?

That these terms have still so much superstitious theological power that for the present it is dangerous to employ them publicly. Public opinion must pass through the purgatory of Atheism and Materialism before it is fit for metaphysics without theology. But my reply was that the *New Age* could not be said to be an organ of the public opinion of to-day, but of the public opinion of to-morrow. Our readers, in fact, have crossed the Red Sea of Materialism and the Jordan of Atheism. We can therefore safely employ the old traditional terms with a purified meaning. 'Guild' we can say without arousing the evil associations of the word, and likewise 'God' and the 'soul' are open now for us to employ without superstition.

But are the meanings attachable to these terms definite?

They are now, though, of course, they have not been for several centuries. The last person in Europe to employ the words 'God' and the 'soul' as exact terms was probably Aquinas. After him the deluge! Luther, I am convinced, had no more exact conception of what he meant by 'God' than had General Booth. Both men were secretly anthropomorphic. And these, you will observe, are the relatively classic deists: I mean that they did insist on a clear image. The remaining body of believers, on the other hand, were too sophisticated to regard God as a man, and too unmetaphysical to regard God clearly as an idea. In consequence, they swam in a fog, and saw God and the soul as bog-lights, will-o'-the-wisps, wreaths of smoke, and finally as nothing at all. For them God and the soul had ceased to have any real existence: the words were empty. But we have now returned, I think, to the possibility of definition—definition that really does define. There is nothing vague, for example, in the definition of 'God' as the 'cause of the original dispositions of matter'. You may say, if you like, that there is nothing necessarily comfortable in it, nothing essentially beneficent, nothing, in fact, traditionally associated with the theological God. On the contrary, I find in the native dispositions of matter everything, save one thing—namely, the 'soul'.

And your definition of the soul, if I remember, is consciousness, or that which becomes aware of the manifestation of the dispositions of matter?

Yes, that is right; but you will realize the difficulty of obtaining a clear conception of this, since we are it. The soul cannot know itself, since it cannot be both the subject and object of knowledge simultaneously. As well ask a man to stand upon his own shoulders or a bird to fly over itself as the soul to be an object of its own knowledge. The knower always remains unknown to himself.

But in that event the soul must always remain unknown!

By no means. In the first place there is a form of knowledge which does not require both a subject and an object. It is knowledge by immediacy. What we ordinarily call knowledge is the sum of our deductions from sense impressions: that is, it is derived not immediately, but mediately, through a chain of impression and deduction. But there is this other means of knowledge which dispenses with one or more or, in the end, with *all* the intermediaries. Intuition, for example, dispenses with one of the ordinary steps; genius dispenses with two; but what the saints called illumination dispenses with all. Secondly, as we cannot look directly at the sun, but may gaze on its reflection in water, or even in the moon, so, I believe, the soul is reflected in the mind, and may be intermediately and, of course, only partially known by this means. At least, it is evident that there is more in the mind than sense-impression has put there.

What, for example?

Well, without raising the controversial ghost of the origin of reason (which, by the way, I cannot regard, as the current psychologists regard it, as an evolutionary outcome of instinct), I will indicate what, in my opinion, the mind owes to the shining proximity of the soul. The desire and the hope of immortality are, of course, unquestionable. No animal entertains them. On the other hand, it has been argued that the hope of immortality which the human mind entertains is a mere balance to the human fore-knowledge of mortality, a fore-knowledge unpossessed by the animals also. But I find this immortal longing so enwoven with other qualities and powers of mind that to regard it as a mere counterbalance of our fore-knowledge of physical death is impossible. On the contrary, every noble quality which distinguishes the human race is derived from the belief in the immortality of the soul.

But even if this were the case, the truth of immortality would not be established, would it?

Agreed; but remember that what we are now seeking is a reflection in the mind of the nature of the soul. We are not asking for an intellectual conception capable of rational demonstration. From the rational point of view, the truth of immortality can only be established by the medium of sense-impressions; and since these are for the present out of the question, immortality is rationally undemonstrable. On the other hand, we have to account for the presence of the belief in the mind at all. To employ an old illustration, if a pure crystal suddenly appears scarlet, we conclude that a scarlet object has been placed near it, and has become reflected in the crystal. Similarly, if a belief appears in the mind without any sensible origin, we may conclude, may we not, that it is due to the contiguity of some non-sensible object? The reflection of the soul in the mind, I maintain, arouses in the latter a belief in immortality—a belief not founded on reason and not derived from sense-impressions, but a belief nevertheless.

But in many instances there is no such belief in the mind. Are we to conclude that, unless the belief in immortality exists in the mind, the soul of the man is afar off or entirely absent?

That need not necessarily be concluded, I think. Very much more may exist in the mind than is dreamt of by the articulate consciousness. The sum of our formulated beliefs may be, and usually is, far less than the sum of the beliefs on which we habitually act. In many instances, indeed, we actually deny in words what our deeds prove we hold in fact. And this accounts, perhaps, both for the noble conduct of professed atheists and materialists and the ignoble conduct of many professed believers in the immortality of the soul.

Then, actually, you do not attach much importance to belief?

Not to beliefs usually articulated. A man's verbal creed may have no real relation with the creed on which he acts. It is a very rare mind that believes what it does, and does what it actually believes. But only in such a mind are thought, feeling, and action really one.

Allowing, then, that the report of the mind is not usually to be relied upon, what evidence is there that the soul really operates on or through the mind? If the mind is not necessarily aware of it, how can anybody be aware of it?

I have said that there are the two means: the first is by immediacy, and the second is by a kind of induction. It is possible, I believe, for the soul to know itself by an act of immediacy which for the moment we may call realization. But it is also possible to discover the soul and even to learn its nature by examining its effects on the mind. We must ask ourselves what qualities exist in the mind that appear to have a non-sensible origin; and, secondly, we may conclude from those qualities the nature of the power or soul that produces them there.

M

VI

WE MODERNS

VI

WE MODERNS

Mr. Edward Moore[1] has published a notebook under the title of *We Moderns*. If you regard it as an imitation of Nietzsche, you must admit that it is, as a *tour de force*, parody of the very highest order, parody amounting to originality almost equal to Nietzsche's own; as good as Burke on Bolingbroke. If you regard it as the notebook of a man hitherto unknown as a writer, you must marvel at the finish of so much of the style—a finish without any superior in its contemporary school. Or, if you take it merely as the occasional reflections of a modern mind, you must be moved to admiration by the variety, the profundity and the passion of the thoughts so apparently easily poured out. Only in one respect do I myself find the work wanting in the qualities that go to make a masterpiece: it is without common sense. The others it has, but this it has not—the obviousness of the perfectly true, the simplicity of the revealed commonplace, the touch of nature that keeps all minds kin.

I am sure that Mr. Moore will not attribute to my remarks a want of respect for himself and his work, more especially when I go on to explain it. Common sense, in my personal vocabulary, is something as far removed from the common as the centre of the world of thought from the circumference. What I imply by it is a grip upon reality

[1] Better known under his real name, Edwin Muir.

which never weakens, even when the substance under one's hand is of the very thinnest. In the simplest form I should say that common sense is the successful resolution of the mind to hold nothing as true that is not implicit in the common mind. John Smith is, in my conception of common sense, the criterion of truth. By whatever road thought travels, and however gorgeous may be the intellectual scenery on the way (and I like as much as any one to be intellectually entertained en route), I require that when it reaches home it shall really find itself at home. Its golden wings, when they are at rest, shall show the marvellous bird that has sailed the empyrean to be, after all, a bird of the earth, a home-bird; and all the truths which shone as it flew, and which in its flight it sang, should reveal themselves as truisms. The brilliant common sense to which I have often referred as the ambition of the *New Age* is not, in my interpretation, the discovery of anything new: it is the re-discovery of what everybody knows but needs to be reminded that he knows. Its method may be difficult; the processes of re-discovery may be complex; but, in the end, its results are, as it were, foregone conclusions, conclusions to which, implicitly if not explicitly, the common mind had already come.

Before considering in what respects Mr. Moore's conclusions appear to me to be lacking in common sense (common sense, by the way, is the mind of democracy—a remark to be remembered in reading Mr. Moore's allusions to democracy), I propose to extend the present introductory digressions by a note or two. To prove that I mean nothing uncomplimentary to Mr. Moore, I shall say that to my mind no writer and thinker that ever lived is so lacking in common sense as Nietzsche, and it cannot be unflattering to Mr. Moore to be put into the same boat with his master! Other writers, scarcely more common sense in my judgement than Nietzsche, are Carlyle, Emerson, Heraclitus (whom Mr. Moore mentions after Nietzsche with profound obeisance), Hegel—in fact, a large proportion of the great Germans—Shaw, Wilde, and many another: all of them considerable if not great minds, and all of them, in my opinion, lacking in the quality of common sense. The absence of common sense is not, therefore, by any means incompatible with power of mind; power of mind is, indeed, very often the cause of the lack of common sense; for it is easy enough for a mind to arrive at common-sense conclusions when it has not the power to arrive at conclusions of its own. But it is much more difficult for an extraordinary mind to be ordinary. My own rule in the matter is simple. It consists in requiring of every conclusion to which I am brought that it shall be *susceptible* of being expressed in what is called plain language, that is, in idiom. I do not care, mind you, in what form the thinker leaves the impression of his thought; it may be in the form of a play by Shakespeare, a dialogue by Plato, a poem by Milton, an essay by Swift, an epic by Homer or Vyasa, or a system of philosophy by Thomas Aquinas. The richer the expression, in fact, the more dignity is lent to the conclusions. But when the conclusions that are contained within the expression are examined, they should be, as I have said, susceptible of being expressed in idiomatic terms. At bottom, it is obvious that all expressed thought is addressed to the jury of mankind and is (if Mr. Durran will permit me to say it) a species of advocacy. The intention of convincing the jury of mankind that such and such a conclusion is correct, or such another conclusion incorrect, may not be openly affirmed by the advocate; it may not even be deliberate and explicit in his own mind; but nevertheless, it is present and operative, and I have no kind of doubt that every published work of thought is propagandist, consciously or unconsciously. But this bears again upon what I have been saying, namely, that every piece of work should reduce to a simple truth capable of being understood by the jury of mankind. For what is the use when addressing a jury whose verdict in your favour you desire, of arriving at a conclusion to which, if even they understood it, they could not assent? The greatest writers and thinkers, I affirm, have always the jury of mankind in their minds as not merely the auditors but as the assessors of the case being put before them. To be sure, the greatest thinkers have also thoughts upon which it is impossible for common sense to pass judgement to-day: thoughts which it is perhaps not yet possible to reduce to truisms. But these, in my experience, the greatest thinkers carefully refrain from putting forward as conclusions: they leave them as myths, as guesses, as poetry or what not. Such, however, of their conclusions as *can* be expressed in plain terms always turn out to be the conclusions of common sense; and by that test they stand.

I see that I shall exceed my space before discussing Mr. Moore in even his outlines. Let me hurry on. To put it very summarily, Mr. Moore is a romantic to whom it is fatal to apply the criterion of common sense. The world in which his discoveries are made is not the world in which the jury of mankind sits: it is a world shared mainly by himself and Nietzsche, a world of his intellectual imagination, a world constructed with *some* of the material of our world, but of a good deal more of the material of his own fancy. In that world of his, neither the problems nor the values are those which are known to us: they are either new in themselves or they exist under novel conditions. It is, for example, a condition of his world that there shall be no fixed values in it, but that the value of everything shall be arbitrarily imposed by what he calls the creative will of man. Obviously this is not our world in which, willy-nilly, man finds himself subject to a scale of values (or, if you like, needs), the fixed degrees of which he is unable to change by a hair's breadth. Nor, again, is the world in which man is a creator the same

world as our own in which man is only a pro-creator. It is
here that the romanticism of Mr. Moore is most plainly
revealed; for it is of the very essence of romanticism to wish
for another kind of world than this which is. To the romantic
not only is this world as it appears not interesting enough,
not good enough, but he has the adventurous courage to
'will' it to be otherwise. Why should I not, he asks? The
world is plastic to the imagination; it is what it is because
imagination has wished it to be so; what if a new imagination
should make a new world of it? Everything for the romantic
turns, you see, upon the plasticity of 'reality', and upon its
responsiveness to the 'creative' will and imagination of man.
Acceptance of the doctrine of Becoming is as inevitable to
the romantic as rejection of the doctrine of Being. Being—
the fixity of what is, and implying unalterability by man's
imagination—is the very devil for the romantics who see in
fixed 'truths' nothing more than 'stagnant values', that is to
say, old imaginations become conventions. Away with
them, they say; 'stagnant values', to quote Mr. Moore, 'are
incompatible with the creative impulse'; they put a bound
to the imagination of man beyond which he cannot 'create'.
Anything 'given' in the nature of the world, and therefore
unalterable by man, shares the same fate at their hands.
'Original Sin', for example, implying a fact (that is, a thing
done once and for all), is anathema to them. Why should
we accept this fact, they say, as a fixed principle, when
plainly it is a theory, an interpretation, a valuation only?
Examine its origin—did it not arise in a misunderstanding?
Was it more than a guess at truth? Had not circumstances
to do with its enunciation? And Mr. Moore replies trium-
phantly that the doctrine of Original Sin 'was itself man's
Original Sin'. In other words, it is not a fixed fact, but an
old theory. It is the same with Christianity, and with all the
doctrines of Christianity. The defect of Christianity, for
Mr. Moore, is that it enunciates fixed 'truths', truths that

were in the beginning, are now and ever shall be. Thus it limits the possible, since only those things are possible that are within the compass of the fixed truths. Away, therefore, with Christianity, says Mr. Moore! Christianity is reaction: it is the clinging of the mind to old formulæ. *Our* problem is 'the enlargement of the field of choice'—and how is this field to be enlarged if we admit the existence of fixed truths? Thus Mr. Moore continues in his iconoclastic career, hammering away at anything that claims to be fixedly true, and urging the transience of every theory. What we need, he says, is a perpetual revaluation of values. Nothing is true for all time; the truth-making faculty must be in perpetual motion, continually making true new valuations and thus continually creating the future. For the future is only fixed if we allow it to be fixed. Our will can create it in our own imagination.

I call all this romantic because, as I have said, it assumes the absence from the world of reality of anything inherent and outside of man's power. It is an affirmation of the infinite alterability of the world. It is in contrast, therefore, with common sense, which, while not denying that the world is alterable, affirms that it is alterable only within fixed limits. There is a perfection possible for common sense, but it is the perfection of things which now are into what they may become. Beyond their own ripeness they cannot pass, for other than what is *possible* to them they cannot become. The Doctrine of Becoming, in the Platonic sense of the word, is not that of Nietzsche or of his disciple Mr. Moore; it is not the Becoming of Things subject to the creative power of man, but the Becoming of Things subject to the pro-creative power of man. For, once again, man is not the creator of the world or of the future of the world, but only, at best, their pro-creator. From this point of view—the classic as opposed to the romantic—there are not only fixed truths, there are no other kinds of truth. Intellect is our organ for the discovery of them; and morality is our method of making use of them. Morality is thus not the will to power or the will to create new values; it is simply working within fixed limits for the perfection of what is. Morality is a universal law. A rose-tree that brings its roses to perfection is a moral bush. A man who does his duty is a moral man and brings forth fruit meet for perfection. Is it not significant that Mr. Moore never once discusses the nature of Duty? Without fixed truths there can be no Duty.

VII

FROM
THE NEW ENGLISH WEEKLY

VII

FROM

THE NEW ENGLISH WEEKLY

At the Newspaper Press Fund the other evening Mr. Neville Chamberlain referred to the 'formidable competition' of the Radio with the Press for the formation of public opinion. The President of the Institute of Journalists afterwards made light of it, and saw in the challenge only a stimulus to better and brighter journals. But is that, indeed, all? Everybody will remember that almost exactly the same was said of the Stage when the 'formidable competition' of the Cinema first began to make itself felt. The Play proper would only be inspired by the challenge to brighter and better plays: the Stage could not be driven to take the second place. But how far has that optimism been justified by events? Where is the Stage to-day, not only in relation to the Cinema but in relation to its own past? Very far from having been inspired to brighter and better plays by the competition of the Cinema, the Stage has largely given up the contest and bound itself to the chariot wheels of its conqueror. Fewer and fewer plays to-day are written or produced for the Stage alone, or even for the Stage primarily. More and more are simply rehearsals for Hollywood.

It is very likely, I think, that on the plane of the Radio and the Press we are going to witness a similar conclusion of the contest. Already the Radio has a larger circulation than any newspaper, and very soon, there is little doubt, its circulation will be greater than that of all the newspapers put together. Is that not certain to subordinate the Press to the Radio as an engine for the formation of public opinion? And must not the Press in consequence take a back seat to the Radio? What is more, I do not see any possible improvement in the Press to give it a hope of triumph over its rival. The Stage always had, and still has, a unique virtue to exploit that would have left the Cinema panting somewhat ridiculously behind it. I cannot imagine, for instance, that the Greek dramatists would have been much perturbed by the competition of such a rival; or that Shakespeare and the Elizabethans, had they been alive to-day, would not have 'thought of something' with which to ensure the supremacy of the Stage. The triumph of the Cinema over the Stage, in fact, has been and is due less to the difference of their intrinsic values than to the superiority of the brains put into the Cinema over those put into the Stage. But in the case of the newspaper Press, it has not, I think, a tuck to run out like the Stage. It has no great past of which to make a great future. Its present will prove, I believe, to be its greatest past, and its future will be a slow decline in relation to the rapid rise of the Radio. For Radio, it is certain, is only in its mighty beginning. There are worlds before it to conquer of which print can scarcely dream. I do not put it beyond the power of Radio to give us, and before long, not only the news of the day, but the news of all the events that have ever occurred. In a universe of curved space in which vibrations are eternal, everything that has ever happened is still happening; and if Radio can already pick out, pick up and transmit news from the still vex'd Bermoothes, I see no reason why eventually it may not give us news of, say, the victory of Salamis. No 'better and brighter' Press could compete with that.

With a little real imagination, it is not difficult to establish something like a parallel between what is happening to-day

and what happened when letters were first invented. Before
the ingenious Kadmus, or whoever it was, devised a script
for the recording of speech, men had for thousands of years
been content to be Speakers and Hearers. Their speech,
moreover, was not confined to the commonplaces of daily
life: it was cultivated as an art. And there is plenty of evidence
to prove that in every form of verbal composition the
predecessors of the 'Yankee' invention of script created
masterpieces with which, as yet, no written substitutes can
compare. The demands on the artist in words in days before
script were far more exacting than the demands made on
the writer of to-day. He had his audience there before him
ready to give him the bird at any moment. He had to appear,
at least, to be improvising even if he had composed and
memorised his speech or narrative or what not weeks in
advance. Above all, he had to be able to capture, hold and
direct the attention and sympathy of his listeners by the use
of his personality, his presence and the range and power of
his vocal and other resources. These demands, taken together,
called for a Man. You cannot conceive of Homer or Vyasa
getting away with it on the presence, let us say charitably,
of a Quartier Latin littérateur. Before script, artists in words
had also to be artists in life; and no degree of verbal finesse,
I think, would have been able to persuade a seeing audience
to believe its ears against all the rest of its senses. Script,
however, won in the end—to the loss of human culture.
The machine triumphed, and with its triumph the great
traditions of improvisation in the speech of man and in all
the provinces of the art of words—narrative, oratory, poetry,
drama—(for it must be remembered that even drama was
improvised before the relatively decadent days of the
scriptorial Greeks)—all came to an end. For the Speaker
there was substituted the Writer, and for the Hearer the
Reader, with such corruptions of integrity and judgement
on both sides that even to-day, after two thousand years of

N

its use, the written word is more often a source of mutual misunderstanding than of common understanding. In two thousand years there have been scarcely a dozen literary critics as good as any 'hearer' of the days before script. Still, to-day, the printing machine 'puts across' writers who, as speakers, would not have been given a first, let alone a second, hearing; and still, to-day, not one reader in a million 'listens' to the printed word as if it were, what it is, a man speaking through a machine, and to be judged as a man speaking. It is possible that the Radio, by partially, if not completely, restoring the original relationship of Speaker, Listener, may at the same time improve both writing and reading. Unless, in fact, it does, I can see Literature going the way of the Stage and of the Press.

Mr. Arnold Bennett's 'Journals' are, of course, a portrait of the man, but drawn by himself in the dark. In spite of all his apparent insight into the character of others and his genuine efforts to be honest with himself, he never saw himself as other than the reflection he was looking for; he never saw himself as somebody else. Even had he done so, however, I doubt whether he would have judged himself correctly. There were certain qualities and defects which Arnold Bennett was blind to. Mr. E. F. Benson quotes as the most revealing of the entries in Bennett's 'Journals' a passage in which he confesses that he did not like to think of himself as 'dependent spiritually, even to a slight degree, on anyone'; but Mr. Benson, I think, has missed the point of the confession, namely, that it was made, not in a spirit of regret, but rather of self-satisfaction. The reason for both the statement and the pride in it was very simple. All his life, from childhood to his death, Arnold Bennett never met anybody, man or woman, whom he instinctively and whole-heartedly admired. It was not that he was always on the watch for the seamy side of the people he met. He was really a most kindly man. But it was the fact that, through no unwillingness of his own, but by simple inability to feel, or by the mischance of never meeting anybody who commanded his complete admiration, he lived and died without the personal experience of worship. As nobody can be an artist who is incapable of worship, or is without the experience of it, and, moreover, certain ranges of perception and understanding are thereby placed beyond his reach, Arnold Bennett's work suffered equally with his life. His characters, equally with himself, were set in a wrong, or, at least, a narrow perspective.

Frank Harris, with whom for some reason Arnold Bennett's name is sometimes coupled, was a greater artist in both life and letters than Bennett. Let us agree that he often gave the impression of being a bounder; but at least he was aware of it. Talking with me one day he asked me if I knew the three ways of making money in London. One was blackmail, one was 'Daily Mail', and the third was whitemail. 'And I am a whitemailer', he added. He then explained the term with a reference to a recent deal he had made with the proprietor of a notorious journal. 'Old D——', he said, 'blackmailed Lord X, and I whitemailed D.' In short, he got half the plunder. It was characteristic of him to defend himself by some such casuistry, since he really could not admit his lapses. He claimed to be an adventurer with a dash of genius who lived by his wits and thought well of himself for doing so. He had the innocence of a boy hi-jacker who preyed on bootleggers, but would have scorned to plunder honest men of letters; a sort of Robin Hood—only that the poor came off rather badly, as I've no doubt they did with Robin Hood.

The jubilee of the Society for Psychical Research will, no doubt, create more stir than the report of the case of

Mrs. Meurig Morris. There is no sympathy, of course, between Psychical Research and Spiritualism, and in the early days of the Society, at any rate, there was hostility rather than sympathy. Prolonged investigation of psychical phenomena, however, was bound to break down a good many prejudices; and the completely sceptical and unconquerably unconvincible members were bound sooner or later to drop out, leaving the Society scarcely distinguishable from a group of scholarly Spiritualists. It is strange how little ice the Society nowadays and Spiritualism itself cut with 'public opinion'. I am told that there are at least thirty thousand professing Spiritualists in this country, with thousands more partially or actively desirous of being convinced. They number among them, moreover, men as great as Sir Oliver Lodge, whose recent letter to the *Times* on the subject of the Physical Universe, in which he summarized the history of Physics from Newton to Einstein, was a masterpiece of lucidity, logic and common sense. In all literature I do not know an abler survey of a tremendous subject. All the same, even such a Triton has failed to convince 'public opinion' that there is anything certain in Spiritualism; and I confess that not for the first time public opinion appears to me to be right. I have dabbled in Spiritualism myself and was, in fact, an active member of the Society for Psychical Research. I have read, I suppose, more than most 'experts', in both Oriental and Occidental mysticism, occultism and spiritism. After years of search and research, my conclusion upon the three greatest and most important questions—survival after death, immortality, the meaning and aim of existence—is that I do not know. The worst of it is that I do not know either whether anybody has ever possessed such knowledge, or even whether such knowledge is possible. I have no evidence to convince me of any of these things. In these circumstances the jubilee of the Society for Psychical Research and all the talk about

Spiritualism leave me cold. I have seen more, heard more, experienced more, than the majority of their members ever will; and still I do not *know* more of the only three matters that ultimately interest man.

.   .   .   .   .

Meanwhile the garden must be cultivated, though again, I do not know, I only feel, the necessity. And I can see no better patch, save ourselves individually, to work upon than the community in which we happen to live. There can be no doubt that society, principally our own nation, plays an overwhelming part in the determination of our mentality no less than our physique; and there is equally no doubt that just as in conditions of depression the physical health of the nation suffers cruelly, so in conditions of social injustice the psyche of the nation is distorted in at least an enormous percentage of its individuals. The result is that in an unjust order of society, practically every individual is abnormal, either from consciously or unconsciously abetting the injustice or from consciously or unconsciously resenting and combatting it. Yet what is there to be done, but to try to establish justice, if only in the interest of our successors, and to try to do it without too much resentment, too much egotism and too much ambition. Without a little of each of these it is probable that no reformer would raise a finger for society. With too much he becomes a curse. It is necessary to find the objective mean between these subjective extremes.

.   .   .   .   .

This leads me to say that I hope many readers of these pages are following the 'Chronicles of Palmerstown' as recorded, in this objective spirit, by the for ever anonymous 'Conclavist'. Very few people have hearts big enough to identify them with suffering or gladness on a world-scale; in all human history there are not more than can be counted on the fingers of one hand. Almost as few can suffer or rejoice with their nation or with their city or even with their class or with their friends. I doubt, indeed, whether very many can disinterestedly suffer or rejoice with anybody but themselves, with, perhaps, at moments or for short periods, one or two other persons. But, at any rate, as a beginning, it is good to attempt to realize the suffering of England under the Norman Deflation on the scale of a single small city such as Palmerstown or Jarrow. The statistics compiled with so much loving care, and verified on the spot by 'Conclavist', will leave nobody cold who is not dead-hearted or not yet fully alive.

The legend of Poe in French criticism, it seems, is not only an exaggeration of Poe's status in letters, but it has also proved a blind spot in the French view of Baudelaire. French men of letters, even the most admired among them, have failed to recognize the greatness which is in Baudelaire outside his notorious field of poetry to almost exactly the same extent to which they have read a greatness which is not there into the work of Poe; and, I imagine, for the same reason that Byron's romantic figure put dust into the eyes of a considerable number of leading European critics, never forgetting one of the greatest of them all, Dr. George Brandes. The reason, needless to say, is that the French have never been able to appreciate English poetry *critically*. There are, of course, lots of English critics who have no critical appreciation of English poetry themselves. An ear for poetry, even in one's own language—particularly for the inner harmonies of poetry—is so rare a phenomenon that only at most two or three critics in a generation have it; and sometimes, as in America to-day, not one outstanding critic has it. But there is, so to say, a tradition of right understanding in regard to one's own poets that ensures, at least in the long run, a correction of any one generation's blindness, whereas, in the case of a foreign poet—Byron or

Poe in France, for example—an estimate once made usually continues down the ages unchanged. Professor Hughes may be pretty sure that however completely he may establish the superiority of Baudelaire over Poe, and Poe's inferiority to many less famous English poets, French criticism will never change its now traditional valuations. I doubt whether M. Valéry, in fact, will trouble himself to read Poe or Baudelaire again: he will be so certain that French criticism in general, and himself in particular, have them rightly placed for all time. English critics, however, will get some amusement from seeing French criticism made a little ridiculous. There are too many literary Aristides in France.

.   .   .   .   .

Mr. Wyndham Lewis has I don't know how many new books coming out this autumn, and each of them, without any doubt, will make something of a literary sensation. Mr. Wyndham Lewis, in fact, is the only English writer who can still produce a 'sensation'. All the other writers of our immediate generation have long ago shot their bolt: they cannot alarm or even shock us any more. But Mr. Wyndham Lewis, perhaps because as yet nobody quite knows what he is talking about, or because he is obviously still anxious to deliver some message or other, is still capable of creating an expectation and consequently a 'sensation'. He stages some very intriguing titles for his work as well. *The Enemy of the Stars,* though perhaps only a paraphrase of *The Apes of God,* carries a promise and a threat that very few young imaginative readers will be able to resist. *The Old Gang and the New Gang,* and *A Tip from the Augean Stable,*—also to be published this autumn by Mr. Desmond Harmsworth,—likewise have titles that should be 'selling'. But whether, when all these books have appeared, Mr. Wyndham Lewis will still have sensationability left, I'm sure I do not know. Carlyle never said all he had to say in thirty volumes, and continued to astonish England to the last. Despite his present autumnal output of six or seven or eight works, Mr. Wyndham Lewis may still, for all anybody knows, be only getting up steam for their successors.

．　　　．　　　．　　　．　　　．

I'm alarmed for his fate, I must confess, by the effect of his Works on his critics. They go into ecstasies scarcely distinguishable in symptoms from St. Vitus's Dance. The best wine doesn't make you drunk, but only quietly clairvoyant; and I suspect the vintage when its indulgents reel off extravagant praise of it. Of *The Apes of God*, for example, Mr. L. A. G. Strong says that it 'belongs to the race of giants'; Mr. Richard Aldington says 'it is one of the most tremendous farces ever conceived in the mind of man'; and Mr. L. P. Hartley says that 'it is like Ulysses deriding Polyphemus, a joke too heroic for mortal minds'. Miracles, of course, do happen: Shakespeare was one of them; Swift was another; and there were great men before Agamemnon. But I have more than my doubts whether the literary miracle implied by these phrases and praises has really occurred in just our particular day and generation. I become a little more sceptical, too, when I look at the company in which this 'giant' is placed. 'You look up at it [Mr. Wyndham Lewis's work] from a distance, as you look up at *Ulysses* or the whole achievement of D. H. Lawrence,' says Mr. Strong. '*The Apes of God*', says Mr. Aldington, 'is the greatest piece of writing since *Ulysses*.' The reference to Mr. Joyce's *Ulysses*, as to a standard, tells us more than all the eulogy itself; it tells us, in fact, precisely what value to attach to it. My doubts of the quality of the vintage are doubled.

．　　　．　　　．　　　．

It becomes necessary sooner or later for every critic of contemporary literature to risk his verdict on certainly the most astonishing literary work of the present century. If Mr. Joyce has done nothing else, he has at any rate created

a touchstone for the literary appreciation of his contemporaries. Merely to dismiss Mr. Joyce as a colossal curiosity
of letters is as idle as to proclaim him a colossus of innovation
whose advent has inaugurated an epoch in literature. No
critic anxious to be right in soul about Mr. Joyce's work—
that is to say, never to have to change his judgement of it—
there being finality in art-judgements as in all others, which
satisfy for ever—can commit himself to opinions such as
these. Mr. Joyce has to be taken more seriously. He has to
be taken rather as one of the 'problems' of contemporary
civilization—a 'problem' like 'Capitalism', let us say. In
Mr. Joyce's work—idea, construction, treatment, vocabulary—the English language itself appears to be exhibiting
the corresponding phenomena of the 'crisis' of industrial
civilization. For the moment, I believe, it is impossible to
say how the chaos will be, or even if it will be, resolved.
The past and the future are at grips for supremacy, and
nobody can be certain which will win. There is much more,
of course, that could be said; but my verdict, all pleadings
taken for granted, is that Mr. Joyce's work is the crisis of
industrial civilization in literature, and will pass with the
crisis, end this how it may.

If man and all his works were to disappear from the
planet, several worlds would disappear at the same time;
and the chief would be the world of language. I am not
referring, of course, to the written word. If the pen is mightier than the sword, the tongue is at least as much mightier
than the pen. Recall that for ages of great culture the pen
did not exist; but the tongue, from all the evidences we have
of its use, must have been cultivated as a superior substitute.
In a thousand ways, indeed, the pen is hopelessly inadequate
to convey the infinite subtleties of speech. Gesture, posture,
tone of voice, facial expression and the movements that
Demosthenes called 'action'—these, together with the effect

of the company of listeners, the setting and the occasion—
how can they ever be conveyed in the record, however art-
fully edited, of the words only, or by verbal description of
what in the original were sensible facts? The despair, however, that every writer must feel of ever producing the
effect of speech is anything but paralysing, except to vanity.
On the contrary, if only because the perfection of speech is
for ever unattainable in the written word, and yet must for
ever constitute the ideal of written perfection, every writer
to whom his art is religious—I mean serious—has a goal,
a guide and a motive, such as, as yet, no other art so clearly
has. In all the plastic arts there is obviously no natural model.
Even in dancing when raised to the Art of Ballet there
exists in nature nothing to which it can compare itself. The
plastic arts and dancing are *models* for life; but the art of the
written word—what we call Literature—is an attempt to
reproduce the life-model of perfected speech.

.   .   .   .   .

I succumb to the temptation to say this for the third time
in the hope that it may then appear as true as it is. And it is
all the more important consciously to realize it to be true
when writers in general have ceased to realize it unconsciously. The eighteenth century of English literature,
beginning with Dryden, was the first period in which the
written English language proper—namely, a blend of
Teutonic and Romance—began to become indubitably
human. In Elizabethan prose there is very little heard of the
human voice. From Dryden onwards, however, the
conscious aim of the greatest writers of English was to make
their written word correspond more and more precisely,
not, of course, to the casually spoken, but to the art-carefully
chosen, spoken word. In a generation or two, what had
begun as a conscious aim had become an unconscious standard; and by the nineteenth century and down to, I should

say, the 'Decadence' of '92, the speech standard of literature was implicitly or explicitly universally accepted.

.   .   .   .   .

The '92's were not, I think, called 'decadent' without good reason. It is absurd, in view of Smollett and Sterne, not to mention Swift, to maintain that it was the morality as expressed in the vocabulary of the '92's that shocked their conservative contemporaries. No doubt many of them thought it was, and tried to discover or to create some evidence for their belief; but the fact is that the 'immorality' of which they were unconsciously aware was a considerably more serious immorality than that of which they thought they were aware. For the immorality of the '92's was not, in fact, an immorality, that is to say, an aberration from the natural norm in life, but in the very essence of the literary art. Elizabethan art was simply a youthful poet singing his way to perfect speech. Dryden, poet and prose-writer too, was the first to be clearly conscious of it. But the '92's, with Walter Pater as the grand initiator, inaugurated a movement in literature not at all in the line of its previous most happily and most naturally established true development towards an always unattainable but an ever nearer identification with speech, but in a direction away from speech into what then began to be called pure literature, literature, that is to say, which aims to become not speech but words. The 'decadent' movement of the '92's was actually, in my judgement, the beginning of our present end. Under the impulse given it by Pater—who, be it remembered, wrote English as if it were a foreign language—literary English began to get further and further away from its natural source and model. To use a violent image constantly employed by America's great living poet-critic, Mr. Robinson Jeffers, written words, after Pater, began to become 'incestuous' and to breed among themselves. Instead of keeping their minds on the unheard discourse of perfect speech, and trying in vain but ever more nearly to write down what their inner, if not outer, ear heard, writers began making patterns among their written words, allowing one to suggest another, mating them together, quite indifferent to their natural relations, by their literary and even their literal associations. The result has been that literature since the '92's has been increasingly sterile in its contact with life. Few writers to-day can produce the effects of speech; and fewer still, either unconsciously or consciously, aim to do so. Apart from journalism, whose language is a bastard of books and the street, most of the written word of to-day is a product of words upon words, books upon books. And it is, without doubt, the most unfruitful age of English literature in respect of its influence upon life. Even unfruitful, unfortunately, is not the truth about it; for its fruit in life is the manifestation of the epicene.

Mr. Julian Huxley used a phrase, 'Reverent Agnosticism', to describe his attitude towards truth, which has been rather deprecated by one of our Views and Reviewers. There must surely, however, have been some misunderstanding to have evoked the criticism. My own avowals of ignorance concerning the three greatest problems for Man—survival, immortality, and the meaning and aim of existence—have been similarly misunderstood; and, I suspect, for the same reason—want of agreement between readers and writers on definitions. The word 'reverent' is obviously a word of emotional content: it is descriptive of a feeling. Equally the word 'agnosticism' refers to experiences of the thinking part of ourselves. Now there is nothing that absolutely requires that what I think and what I feel shall be the same or even similar, though as experiences I may be equally certain of their actuality. Suppose, then, that in relation to the Universe I feel irresistibly and indubitably reverent, while at the same time, to my thinking, its meaning and

aim (if any) are unintelligible, and many of its facts completely unknown—why is not the phrase 'reverent agnosticism' perfectly descriptive of my state? We can agree that
it's a pity, since the difference means either that my thinking
is in advance or in arrears of my feeling; in either case, that
I am not exempt from the damnatory clauses of the Athan-
asian Creed—but who, in the first place, is to say which is
in advance of which; in the second place, which is the better
way to Truth; and, in the third place, how, supposing we
knew, we could change the relation? It seems probable to
me that in all these high matters we are disputing about
algebra without knowing arithmetic. We are arguing about
philosophy and religion before we have even a provisional
common agreement about the very ground and condition
of our human experience—the psychological norm of the
species Man.

The *Modern Scot* devotes a considerable part of its Summer
issue to a centenary commentary on Scott by various
hands—Edwin Muir, Rebecca West, Donald Carswell, and
A. T. Cunninghame.

Some very just comments are made upon Scott as a writer
by the contributors I have named. They seem all to agree
that Scott is not, and never was, what he was; that he never
took writing as a high artistic mission, that he was not truly
romantic, that he avoided exposing the core of life, 'believ-
ing it to be awful' (Rebecca West), and that, in sum, he is
no longer read or worth reading. But, with the exception
of Mr. Cunninghame, none of the critics fastens securely
upon the greatness of Scott, or, indeed, seems to be clearly
aware of it. And Mr. Cunninghame himself, strangely and
even shockingly enough, is aware of it only to belittle it.
'Not only', he says, 'is Scott a household word in Scotland,
—and he might have added 'the whole world'—but 'his
characters have such an existence in the popular mind that

there are none, or few of us, whether or not we have read the Waverley Novels, who do not know Dugald Dalgetty, Bailie Nicol Jarvie, Ivanhoe, Dandie Dinmont, Rob Roy, in the way that we know Mary Queen of Scots and William Wallace'. But let us pause a moment, as Mr. Cunninghame should have paused, but didn't, to realize what is implied in this tribute to Scott. A writer who has succeeded in successfully competing with actual history in the creation of characters so that posterity can scarcely distinguish between the real and the imagined, is not to be relegated at any time to a lower position than the very highest in literature. We will allow that the *rank* of Scott's created characters is not the most elevated. He does not, for example, compare in the quality and greatness of his characters with Homer, whom in many respects he resembled. Still less, of course, was his creation of characters on the plane of the literary creators of the Greek gods—each of whom, as I believe, was originally a character in fiction. But, admitting that his creatures were below the level of real greatness, what genius, what creative stuff, what demi-urgic force, he must have possessed to make them live and move and have their being on equal terms with the creations of Nature. That Dugald Dalgetty and the rest—and many others—are as 'real' as Mary of Scotland and Wallace is a tribute to Scott that Mr. Cunninghame fails to appreciate when he has made it. Who cares about the merely 'literary' influence of Scott as a writer? Who cares whether he was 'modern', like Goethe, in his own day, or that no contemporary writer . . . shows the slightest trace of his influence or the slightest critical interest in his work? To create characters that live is a totally different thing from giving an impetus to a new school of writers, or even from initiating a new school of thought. Scott's order of creative genius was as much above 'literature' as life is above art.

VIII

ON LOVE

ACKNOWLEDGEMENT
The essay ON LOVE is included by kind permission of
The Unicorn Press

VIII

ON LOVE

You must learn to distinguish among at least three kinds
of love (though there are seven in all): instinctive love,
emotional love, and conscious love. There is not much fear
that you cannot learn the first two, but the third is rare and
depends upon effort as well as intelligence. Instinctive love
has chemistry as its base. All biology is chemistry, or perhaps
we should say alchemistry; and the affinities of instinctive
love, manifesting in the attractions, repulsions, mechanical
and chemical combinations we call love, courtship, marriage,
children and family, are only the human equivalents of a
chemist's laboratory. But who is the chemist here? We call
it Nature. But who is Nature? As little do we suspect as
the camphor which is married to the banyan suspects a
gardener. Yet there is a gardener. Instinctive love, being
chemical, is as strong, and lasts as long, as the substances and
qualities of which it is the manifestation. . . . These can be
known and measured only by one who understands the
alchemical progression we call heredity. Many have remarked that happy or unhappy marriages are hereditary.
So, too, are the number of children, their sex, longevity, etc.
The so-called science of astrology is only the science (when
it is) of heredity over long periods.

Emotional love is not rooted in biology. It is, in fact, as
often anti-biological in its character and direction. Instinctive
love obeys the laws of biology, that is to say, chemistry,
and proceeds by affinities. But emotional love is often the

o

mutual attraction of disaffinities and biological incongruities. Emotional love, when not accompanied by instinctive love (as it seldom is), rarely results in offspring; and when it does, biology is not served. Strange creatures arise from the embraces of emotional love, mermen and mermaids, Bluebeards and des belles dames sans merci. Emotional love is not only short-lived, but it evokes its slayer. Such love creates hate in its object, if hatred is not already there. The emotional lover soon becomes an object of indifference and quickly thereafter of hatred. These are the tragedies of love emotional.

Conscious love rarely obtains between humans; but it can be illustrated in the relations of man to his favourites in the animal and vegetable kingdoms. The development of the horse and the dog from their original state of nature; the cultivation of flowers and fruit—these are examples of a *primitive* form of conscious love, primitive because the motive is still egoistic and utilitarian. In short, Man has a personal use for the domesticated horse and the cultivated fruit; and his labour upon them cannot be said to be for love alone. The conscious love motive, in its developed state, is the wish that the object should arrive at its own native perfection, regardless of the consequences to the lover. 'So she become perfectly herself, what matter I?' says the conscious lover, 'I will go to hell if only she may go to heaven.' And the paradox of the attitude is that such love always evokes a similar attitude in its object. Conscious love begets conscious love. It is rare among humans because, in the first place, the vast majority are children who look to be loved but not to love; secondly, because perfection is seldom conceived as the proper end of human love—though it alone distinguishes adult human from infantile and animal love; thirdly, because humans do not know, even if they wish, what is good for those they love; and fourthly, because it never occurs by chance, but must be the subject of resolve, effort, self-conscious choice. As little as Bushido or the Order of Chivalry grew up accidentally does conscious love arise by nature. As these were works of art so must conscious love be a work of art. Such a lover enrols himself, goes through his apprenticeship, and perhaps one day attains to mastery. He perfects himself in order that he may purely wish and aid the perfection of his beloved.

Would one enrol in this service of conscious love? Let him forswear personal desire and preconception. He contemplates his beloved. What manner of woman (or man) is she (or he)? A mystery is here: a scent of perfection the nascent air of which is adorable. How may this perfection be actualized—to the glory of the beloved and of God her Creator? Let him think, is he fit? He can only conclude that he is not. Who cannot cultivate flowers, or properly treat dogs and horses, how shall he learn to reveal the perfection still seedling in the beloved? Humility is necessary, and then deliberate tolerance. If I am not sure what is proper to her perfection, let her at least have free way to follow her own bent. Meanwhile to study—what she is, and may become; what she needs, what her soul craves and cannot find a name, still less a thing, for. To anticipate to-day her needs of to-morrow. And without a thought all the while of what her needs may mean to me. You will see, sons and daughters, what self-discipline and self-education are demanded here. Enter these enchanted woods, ye who dare. The gods love each other consciously. Conscious lovers become gods.

Without shame people will boast that they have loved, do love or hope to love. As if love were enough, or could cover any multitude of sins. But love, as we have seen, when it is not conscious love—that is to say, love that aims to be both wise and able in the service of its object—is either an affinity or a dis-affinity, and in both cases equally unconscious, that is, uncontrolled. To be in such a state of love is to be dangerous either to oneself or to the other or to both. We are then polarized to a natural force (which has its own objects to serve regardless of ours) and charged with its force; and events are fortunate if we do not damage somebody in consequence of carrying dynamite carelessly. Love without knowledge and power is demoniac. Without knowledge it may destroy the beloved. Who has not seen many a beloved made wretched and ill by her or his 'lover'? Without power the lover must become wretched, since he cannot do for his beloved what he wishes and knows to be for her delight. Men should pray to be spared the experience of love without wisdom and strength. Or, finding themselves in love, they should pray for knowledge and power to guide their love. Love is *not* enough.

'I love you,' said the man. 'Strange that I feel none the better for it,' said the woman.

The truth about love is shown in the order in which religion has been introduced into the world. First came the religion of Power, then came the religion of Knowledge, and last came the religion of Love. Why this order? Because Love without the former qualities is dangerous. But this is not to say that the succession has been anything more than discretion: since Power alone, like Knowledge alone, is only less dangerous than Love alone. Perfection demands simultaneity in place of succession. The order is only evidence that since succession was imperative (man being subject to the dimension of Time which is succession), it was better to begin with the less dangerous dictators and leave Love to the last. A certain prudent man, when he felt himself to be in love, hung a little bell round his neck to caution women that he was dangerous. Unfortunately for themselves they took too much notice of it; and he suffered accordingly.

Until you have wisdom and power equal to your love, be ashamed, my sons and daughters, to avow that you are in love. Or, since you cannot conceal it, love humbly and study to be wise and strong. Aim to be worthy to be in love.

All true lovers are invulnerable to everybody but their beloved. This comes about not by wish or effort but by the fact of true, i.e. whole, love alone. Temptation has not to be overcome: it is not experienced. The invulnerability is magical. Moreover, it occurs more often than is usually supposed. Because 'unfaithfulness' is manifested, the conclusion is drawn that invulnerability does not exist. But 'infidelity' is not necessarily due to temptation, but possibly and often to indifference; and there is no Fall where there is no Temptation. Men should learn to discriminate in themselves and in women real and assumed invulnerability. The latter, however eloquent, is due to fear. Only the former is the fruit of love. A certain prudent man, desiring, as all men and women do in their hearts, invulnerability in himself and in the woman he loved, set about it in the following way. He tasted of many women and urged his beloved to taste of many men. After a few years he was satisfied that nothing now could tempt him. She, on the other hand, had had no doubt of herself from the beginning. She had been born invulnerable; he had attained it.

The state of being in love is not always defined in relation to one object. One person has the talisman of raising another to the plane of love (that is, of polarizing him or her with the natural energy of love); but he or she may not be then either the sole beloved or, indeed, the beloved at all. There are, among people as among chemical substances, agents of catalysis which make possible interchanges and combinations into which the catalysts themselves do not enter. Frequently they are unrecognized by the parties affected, and usually by themselves as well. In the village of Bor-na, not far from Lhassa, there once lived a man who was such a catalyst. People who spoke with him instantly fell in love, but not with him, or, indeed, immediately with anybody in particular. All that they were aware of was that they had, after conversation with him, an active spirit of love which was ready to pour itself out in loving service. The European troubadours were perhaps such people.

There is no necessary relation between love and children; but there is a necessary relation between love and creation. Love is for creation; and if creation is not possible, then for procreation; and if even that is not possible, then for creations of which, perhaps fortunately, we are unconscious. Take it, however, as the fundamental truth about Love: that it always creates. Love created the world; and not all its works are beautiful! The procreation of children is the particular function of instinctive love: that is its plane. But above and below this plane, other kinds of love have other functions. Emotional love is usually instinctive love out of place; and its procreations are in consequence misfits in the world. The higher forms of love, on the other hand, either exclude procreation, not artificially but naturally, or include it only as a by-product. Neither the purpose nor the function of conscious love is children; unless we take the word in the mystic sense of becoming as little children. For briefly, the aim of conscious love is to bring about re-birth, or spiritual childhood. Everybody with perceptions beyond those of male and female must be aware of the change that comes over the man or woman, however old in years, who loves. It is usually instinctive; yet it symbolizes the still more marvellous change occurring when a man or woman loves consciously or is aware of being consciously loved. The youth in such cases has all the air of eternity; and it is, indeed, the divine youth. The creation of such a spiritual child in each of the two lovers is the peculiar function of conscious love; and it depends neither upon marriage nor upon children. There are other creations proper to still higher degrees of love; but they must remain until we have become as little children.

We are not one but three in one; and the fact is represented in our physiological make-up. The three main systems,

cerebral, nervous, and instinctive, exist side by side, sometimes appearing to co-operate, but more often failing, and
usually at cross-purposes. In relation to the external world
it depends upon the system in charge of the organism at the
moment what the response to any given stimulus will be.
If the cerebral system is on duty—that is, temporarily in
charge of the organism—the response will be one. If the
nervous or instinctive system is alone awake, the replies
will be different. Three quite different people, each with
his own ideas of how his organism should act, exist in us
at once: and usually they refuse to co-operate with each
other, and, in fact, get in each others' way. Now imagine
such an organism, tenanted by three squabbling persons,
to 'fall in love'. *What* has fallen in love; or, rather, which
of the three? It seldom happens that all three are in love
at the same time or with the same object. One is in love, the
others are not; and either they resist, or, when the lover is
off guard, make his organism unfaithful (driving the poor
lover to lies and deceit or self-reproach); or they are forced
into submission, battered into acquiescence. In such circumstances, which every candid reader will recognize, what is
a lover?

You imagine that you are continent because you have
refrained from sex-relations; but continence is of the senses
as well as of the organs, and of the eyes chiefly. From each
of the senses there streams energy—energy as various as the
man himself. It is not only possible but it is certain that we
can expend ourselves intellectually, emotionally or sexually
through any one of the senses. To look with lust is much
more than simply to look: it is to expend one of the finer
substances of which complete sex-energy is composed:
something passes in the act of vision which is irrecoverable;
and for the want of it the subsequent sex-life is incomplete.
It is the same with the other senses, though less easily realized.
In short, it is possible to become completely impotent by

means of the senses alone—yes, by the eyes alone—while remaining continent in the ordinary meaning of the word.

The chastity of the senses is natural in a few people; but by the many it must be acquired if it is to become common. Under the greatest civilization human history has yet known, the capital of which was the city whose poor remains are Bagdad, the chastity of the senses was taught from early childhood. Each sense was carefully trained; and exercises were devised to enable pupils to discriminate the different emanations arriving from sense perceptions intellectually, emotionally, instinctively or erotically motived. From this education people acquired the power of directing their senses, with the result that chastity was at least possible, since it was under control. Eroticism thereby became an art, in the highest form the world has seen. Its faint echoes are to be found in Persian and Sufi literature to-day.

Bluebeard and La Belle Dame are the male and female types respectively of the same psychology—inspirers of hopeless because unrequitable passion. The decapitated ladies who hung round Bluebeard's chamber were really about his neck; and they had only to let go to be free. Similarly the pale warriors and princes in the cave of La Belle Dame were there by choice, if an irresistible attraction can be called choice. The legends present Bluebeard and La Belle Dame from the point of view of their escaped victims, that is to say, as monsters delighting in erotic sacrifice. But both were as much victims as their titular victims; and both suffered as much, if not more. In such cases of uncontrolled attraction, power passes through the medium, who thus becomes formidably magnetic; and men and women in sympathetic relation are drawn towards him or her like filings towards a magnet. At first, no doubt, the experiences of a Bluebeard or La Belle Dame are pleasant and fortifying to self-pride and self-vanity. The other sex is at their feet. But when, having realized that the power is neither their own nor under their control, they discover that they too are victims, the early satisfaction is dearly paid for. The cure for all parties is difficult. It consists in the re-education of the body and the senses.

Love without divination is elementary. To be in love demands that the lover shall divine the wishes of the beloved long before they have come into the beloved's own consciousness. He knows her better than she knows herself; and loves her more than she loves herself; so that she becomes her perfect self without her own conscious effort. *Her* conscious effort, when the love is mutual, is for him. Thus each delightfully works perfection in the other.

But this state is not ordinarily attained in nature: it is the fruit of art, of self-training. All people desire it, even the most cynical; but since it seldom occurs by chance, and nobody has published the key to its creation, the vast majority doubt even its possibility. Nevertheless it is possible, provided that the parties can learn and teach humbly. How to begin? Let the lover when he is about to see his beloved think what he should take, do, or say so as to give her a delightful surprise. At first it will probably be a surprise that is not a complete surprise: that is to say, she will have been aware of her wish, and only delighted that her lover had guessed it. Later the delightful surprise may really surprise her; and her remark will be: 'How did you know I should be pleased, since I should never have guessed it myself?' Constant efforts to anticipate the nascent wishes of the beloved while they are still unconscious are the means to conscious love.

Take hold tightly; let go lightly. This is one of the great secrets of felicity in love. For every Romeo and Juliet tragedy arising from the external circumstances of the two parties, a thousand tragedies arise from the circumstances created by the lovers themselves. As they seldom know the moment or the way to 'take hold' of each other, so they even more rarely know the way or the moment to 'let go'. The ravines of Mount Meru (i.e. Venusberg) are filled with lovers who cannot leave each other. Each wishes to let go, but the other will not permit it. There are various explanations of this unhappy state of affairs. In most instances the approach has been wrong: that is to say, the parties have leapt into union without thought of the way out. Often the first five minutes of the lovers' *first* meeting are decisive of the whole future of the relations. In some instances the original relation has been responsible for the subsequent difficulty of 'letting go': it should never have been; or not have been in the precise circumstances of its occurrence. Mistimed relations always cause trouble. In other cases the difficulty is due to difference in age, education, or 'past'. One is afraid to 'let go' because it appears to be the last hope, or because too much time has already been spent on it, or because it has been the best up to date, or because his 'ideal', created by education, demands eternal fidelity even where it is not possible, because it is not desired by both; or because one is over-sensitive from past experience and cannot face another failure, or because the flesh being willing the spirit is weak, i.e. neither party can use a knife; or because circumstances are unfavourable, i.e. the parties must continue to see each other; or because of imagination, as when one or the other pictures the happiness of the other without him or her. There are a thousand explanations, and every one of them, while sufficient as cause, is quite inadequate as reason, the fact being that when one of the parties desires to separate, the other's love-duty is to 'let go'. Great love can both let go and take hold.

Jealousy is the dragon in paradise; the hell of heaven; and the most bitter of the emotions because associated with the sweetest. There is a specific against jealousy, namely, conscious love; but this remedy is harder to find than the disease is to endure. But there are palliatives of which the first therapeutic condition is the recognition of the disease and the second the wish to cure oneself. In these circumstances let the sufferer deliberately experiment. Much may be forgiven him or her during this process. He may, for instance, try to forward the new plans of his former beloved—but this is difficult without obvious hypocrisy. Or he may plunge into new society. Or he may engage himself in a new work that demands all his energy. Or he may cast a spell on his memory and regard his former beloved as dead; or as having become his sister; or as having gone away on a long journey; or as having become enchanted. Best, however, if he 'let go' completely with no lingering hope of ever meeting her again.

Be comforted. Our life is but one day of our Life. If not to-day, to-morrow! Let go!

IX

ON RELIGION

IX

ON RELIGION

Suppose that a remote posterity, unversed in mathematics and the scientific research equipment of our age, should inherit one of our current science manuals. There they would read or, rather, decipher, such statements as that light travels at the rate of 186,000 miles a second; that the sun is 92,000,000 miles distant from the earth and that the light of the nearest star takes four and a half light years to reach us. What would they make of it all? Some of them, it is probable, would hold that their forerunners must have possessed a faculty lost to themselves, and in consequence would attach a mystical significance to the unverifiable dogmas; they might even repeat these dogmas as possibly magical formulas. But undoubtedly the best common sense of the day, in the absence of the means, or any conception of the means, of verification, would dismiss the statements as being childish guesses or, at best, as barbarous abracadabra. Only a very few would suspect that perhaps we were not such fools as we appeared, and give us suspended credit for a method behind our madness. But our method itself and the instruments we employ would be still to seek.

The foregoing picture may serve to illustrate what may possibly—let us say no more than possibly—be our very own situation in regard to the ancient 'science' of religion. We have inherited a few of the text-books once circulated among the illuminati of more or less extinct civilizations, and we find them to contain statements of equal exactitude and incredibility concerning things of which we have no verifiable knowledge, as that there is a God Who is a trinity of Persons, Who created the Universe according to Reason, and Man in His own image, and Who placed us in the world with potentialities of consciously becoming like unto Himself. Some of us to-day are disposed, like our imagined descendants, to take these traditional statements mystically; to repeat them as magical formulas; and to assume that a lost faculty, the so-called religious sense, was possessed by our ancestors of ancient Egypt, India, Persia and Syria. So relatively powerful, in fact, are these that their attitude towards the inherited dogmas of ancient religion is still the standard of respectability. The weight of common sense, however, is slowly but surely making itself felt; and the day is not far off when the intelligence of our civilization will explicitly decline even to be interested in grandiose statements apparently insusceptible of proof. Only a few, a very few, will continue to suspect that perhaps the Egyptians, the Buddhists, the Pythagoreans and the Gnostics were people very like ourselves in respect of faculty and unlike us only in the same respect in which we shall differ from a remote posterity without our science, namely, in the possession, not of a lost faculty, but of a lost method or technique. And for these few, too, the method or technique is still to seek—or perchance only to recognize.

Let us assume that we belong to these few and that we begin, at least roughly, to define the conditions essential to our hopeful quest of the lost technique. The first, obviously, is the discrimination of Religion from the subjects with which it has been associated in the course of time. As certainly as our descendants would, if they were so much interested, at least give our Science the distinction of being concerned about some definite field of possible or, maybe, impossible knowledge, and discriminate between our Science and our Ethics, our Science and our Sociology, our Science and our popular customs, so we undoubtedly can at once begin to distinguish in the traditional Religion of our ancient fore-runners certain characteristics unique and peculiar to the subject. Whether verifiable or not, whether even intelligible to us or not, it is clear that the statements concerning Religion contained in the surviving texts assume certain specific generalizations as to the World and Man and, either as cause or as effect, certain specific attitudes and rational obligations laid upon Man himself. Still roughly, they can be said to be as follows: that the Universe is an intelligent and therefore intelligible Cosmos; that the obligation and, at the same time, the highest possible aim of Man is to under-stand and to co-operate with the intelligent laws that govern it; that in order to accomplish this a special way of life or technique is necessary; and that this technique consists primarily in a method of 'divinizing', that is to say, of raising to a higher conscious level Man's present state of being. Everything essential, it seems, to an elementary definition of Religion, as the subject has come down to us, is contained in this brief summary. There is the cosmological element, for instance, missing from our Sociology and Ethics. The cosmology, moreover, differs from the cosmology of our Science in assuming universal psychological values; every-thing is God; and therefore intelligent and potentially intelligible to Reason. Man has a unique and designed place and, therefore, function, in the cosmological scheme. In other words, he enters into obligations by being born. At the same time, his awareness of his place and function is not a gift of nature: he must acquire it by a special effort and by a special method. Finally, both his own development and his own greatest happiness depend upon his discovery of his function and his conscious discharge of it.

This outline is formidable enough to daunt the rational seeker after the rationale of ancient Religion. Without prepossessions for or against these specific dogmas of our

P

forefathers, but with, nevertheless, a benevolent curiosity as to the possible method involved in them, how are we even to begin our search? Certainly there is little in modern Science, or in any branch of it, to provide us with even a hint of a method of verification. Of any means of knowing if an intelligent God exists, our Science is completely and indifferently ignorant; and naturally and consequently all the lesser branches of knowledge, springing from the same trunk, must equally dispense with the hypothesis of God's existence. Equally, too, our current working conceptions must dispense with unproven potentialities such as are assumed in the religious statements concerning Man's possible conscious divinization by understanding, becoming and service. What may be may equally not be; and our Science deals only with potentialities actualized, neither with Reality nor with Potentiality metaphysically, but with Actuality, that is to say, the physical. No exception can be made either in the case of Philosophy or in the case of Psychology. Both are too good pupils of the scientific school to resist for long the full employment of the actualistic method. There linger, it is true, medieval ghosts in both fields who speculate hither and thither in the hope of finding pasture for their souls, but with the increasing chemicalization of psychology, everything dependent upon psychological processes, such, for instance, as speculative philosophy, will more and more lose scientific value, as being insufficiently radical. Sooner or later, the question in regard to every philosophical or psychological opinion will be not its value as an objective statement but its value as merely a symptom of personal chemistry.

With no sure guide in the religious traditions themselves, and with not the least glimmer of light from modern Science, our quest for the possible or not impossible technique employed by our ancestors in formulating their 'dogmas' seems doomed on the threshold of failure. And rationally it must be so. If we cannot accept on faith the doctrines and assumptions specifically associated with Religion, nor can find in modern Science even the end of a clue that promises to reveal it to us, our case is lost from the beginning. And we must reconcile ourselves with Science as we have it and remember only as an ancient dream the faith of our forefathers. By the same token, our dreams of the future must similarly be shepherded through the Gates of Horn. For, with the admission that we neither have discovered nor can begin to discover the yet not impossible technique of religion as formulated by our ancestors, we must deny ourselves the scientific hope of discovery in the future. If modern Science can throw no light on the Religion of the past—on Religion, that is to say, as defined above— neither can it promise us a Religion in the future.

The field of Religion, chimerical or not, can no more be changed than the field of any other department of Science, actual or so-called. Religion, like Ethics or Physics, is, by definition, what it is and always will be. And by declining to be so much as interested in the question of a technique of Religion, Science declares itself bankrupt of Religion forever.

Things, however, are seldom as black as rationalism paints them; and scientists fortunately are not all as scientific as their science. In short, there are loopholes of escape from our impasse; and one of the most promising is to be found in modern psychology; precisely, in fact, in the latest conquest of the scientific method, the field of Behaviourism. Behaviourism, there is no doubt, has come to stay. It is true that Behaviourism is still in little more than the elementary stage, that we have still much to learn and certainly some surprising discoveries to anticipate; but the method that has begun to collect and verify the data of human psychology at its source, that is to say, in observable behaviour beginning with earliest infancy, is assuredly destined to supersede the pseudo-scientific methods of introspection and psycho-analysis. Henceforward for Science there is only one possible approach to Psychology, the approach of observation, verification and experiment. Every other approach is now medieval.

The question, however, is what and whose behaviour we are to observe; or, without prejudice to any other field, the legitimacy of a field of observation which, as we have said, on the face of it appears to promise some light on our inquiry concerning a technique of Religion. To be explicit, is self-observation, together with the usual sequel in the scientific method—verification, hypothesis, experiment and demonstration—equally legitimate with the observation of others; and, if it is, can we devise a method to ensure its rigorous pursuit? Are we ourselves, as behaving organisms, a valid subject for our scientific research—assuming, of course, that we employ the same objective means as we should employ in the case of others? Is self-knowledge at least as possible scientifically as the knowledge of anything else? There can be no doubt of the reply; and Behaviourists, in fact, have admitted it. Though, at the outset, self-observation as a scientific method of research into human psychology labours under both acquired and natural disabilities, as, for example, association with introspection and the presence of the personal equation in its most intimate form, neither its past nor its inherent difficulty can reasonably be said to disqualify it. All that would be necessary would be to be doubly on guard against subjectivity and to be all the more rigorously and objectively scientific in sight of the snares of misunderstanding and self-deception.

That self-observation has at least an affinity with the subject-matter of Religion is obvious by inspection. A characteristic of Religion is concern with oneself next to God. On closer examination, indeed, this self-concern in every possible sense proves to be one of the leading motives and fundamental suppositions of Religion as it has come down to us. The poignancy of religious phraseology concerning the lot and fate of Man, the hopes and fears of his salvation, the speculations concerning the nature of the individual soul, the promises of divinization, all indicate a self-concern not merely instinctive but visceral and cerebral. The individual in Religion is mightily concerned for himself, but for himself in every possible and even impossible way. Everything he does, including not only his acts but his thoughts and feelings, may be and, from the point of view of Religion, is held to be, at least potentially, profoundly significant. The individual's awareness of and concern for himself in the highest possible degree is assumed as one of the very conditions of the religious life.

We may conclude, therefore, that if self-awareness, or, let us say, self-consciousness, is not the sole or main aim of Religion as formulated in our texts, at least it is an implied pre-requisite of the main aim which appears to be the understanding and service of the Creator, God. All the commandments, injunctions and exhortations to God's service already imply knowledge of the means of response and ability to control them; and since, in the last resort, all our responses are only forms of our actual behaviour, the knowledge of our behaviour is a necessary condition of our control of it, assuming for the moment that such control may prove to be possible. To know ourselves as we actually are—that is to say, in our current actual behaviour—may not be, and is not, the object of Religion; but it certainly forms a necessary step to Religion, and, as it would seem, the first necessary step. How can God be served if we are ignorant of the actual present behaviour of the servant? Conscious service implies self-knowledge as well as knowledge of the Being to be served. Self-consciousness or awareness of our actuality is, in short, an indispensable element in Religion as strictly defined.

How did our forefathers, who founded and practised Religion, set about attaining self-knowledge? The answer to this question would throw the first real ray of light on the nature of the Religious technique. But, alas, it is not forthcoming, or forthcoming only in such dark sayings as themselves demand a key that is missing. We hear of schools where 'Mysteries' were taught, of long courses of initiation, of difficult exercises of various kinds; of Masters and pupils. And we can distinguish in the surviving texts words and phrases having the air of an exact but incomprehensible connotation. How many of the words that to-day pass as religious had once a purely technical psychological meaning we cannot guess; but unless we are to attribute to our ancestors a mythical religious sense, it is highly probable that time alone is responsible for their present 'pious' associations. In short, if the preliminary aim of the ancient Religious Schools was the preparation of ordinary men and women for the extraordinary life of conscious co-operation with the Creator, the means employed for the necessary pre-requisite of self-knowledge must have been anything but religious in our modern sense. On the contrary, they must have been practical first and foremost; and in all probability the vocabulary of the technique was chosen from the popular science of the day.

It has been suggested that in the current theories of Behaviourism ancient Religion and modern Science meet. Let us add, however, that they only meet, they do not as yet mingle. Nevertheless, it is in the vocabulary of Behaviour-ism that the technique of self-observation can best be stated; and be the outcome of the technique the re-discovery or confirmation of the ancient dogmas or their dismissal as superstitions, the new field and method of psychological research can at least be said to be promising. What, indeed, can more plainly call for rigorous self-examination than the very instruments upon which all our observations of the rest of the world depend? Behaviourists observing the behaviour of others are still at two degrees from the object nearest them; and the result is infallibly, in consequence, a closer and closer approximation to physics and ultimately to the elimination of psychology altogether. Self-observation of one's own behaviour automatically corrects this fatal error of emptying out the baby with the bath water. While observing, however objectively, my own behaviour, I am under no temptation to forget the accompanying sensations, emotions and trains of thought. I cannot overlook or underrate the psychological element when it obtrudes itself into the very phenomena I am witnessing. And the preservation of my awareness of this concomitant of many forms of my behaviour gives a higher degree of understanding when I apply myself to the observation of others. Once this is realized, the technique of the Behaviourists may be taken straight away and applied without change to our new field. We can accept their classification of forms of behaviour, together, if necessary, with their means of measuring Man. None of their implications, even in the extreme form of organic mechanism, are positively alien to us. If self-observation be the next step in scientific Behaviourism, and it appears logically to be, the second step of Behaviourism may very well prove to be the first step in the technique of Religion.

A warning, however, is necessary. Careful and impartial observation of one's own behaviour would at the first blush appear to be as easy as the observation of the behaviour of others. Far from this, however, is the usual experience of the curious self-observer. In fact, from the very beginning of the collection of such data about one's own actual behaviour, the path is strewn with difficulties of a hitherto unrealized kind. It would almost seem that Nature resents the attempt to observe her in oneself, so powerful and at the same time so subtle is the resistance commonly experienced. Possibly it was this very discovery that led to the formulation of the dogmas of ancient Religion. They had tried to meet themselves, Nature and God, face to face!